THE
MIRACLES

THE
MIRACLES

Understanding
What Jesus Did

GARY INRIG

Our Daily Bread
Publishing™

Interior design by Rob Williams, InsideOut Creative Arts, Inc.

Library of Congress Cataloging-in-Publication Data Available

Printed in the United States of America

21 22 23 24 25 26 27 28 | 8 7 6 5 4 3 2 1

With gratitude to family and the many friends
whose love, encouragement, prayers, and wisdom
have sustained Elizabeth and me through the years.

"A friend loves at all times, and a brother is born for adversity."

(Proverbs 17:17)

CONTENTS

—⟋w⟍—

INTRODUCTION

—ɱ—

CAN WE EVEN BELIEVE IN MIRACLES?

One wintery night in 1804, having finished his work for the day, Thomas Jefferson turned his attention to a project he'd been thinking about for some time. He took out two Bibles and a penknife, or perhaps a razor, and opened both Bibles to the Gospels. Then he began to work systematically through accounts of the Lord's life, cutting out the parts he thought represented the authentic Jesus and pasting them into a kind of scrapbook, while discarding the rest. The result was a book filled with the teachings and some of the actions of Jesus but devoid of any miracles. He had it bound, labeled it "The Philosophy of Jesus of Nazareth," and kept it a closely held secret, aware of the negative political ramifications, should his project be made public.

But sixteen years later, at the age of seventy-seven and retired from public life, he returned to his project. This time he had six Bibles, two in English, two in French, and two in Latin and Greek. He created a new, slightly larger version of his first work, this time laid out in four languages and entitled "The Life and Morals of Jesus Christ." As before, his story ended at Jesus's crucifixion, with no mention of any of the miracles the gospel writers attributed to Jesus.

Jefferson was a deist who claimed to be "a real Christian, that is to say, a disciple of the doctrines of Jesus." He rejected the idea that Jesus was anything more than an excellent man, and claimed the right to pick and choose what in the Gospels was authentic. As he wrote in a letter to John Adams, the worthy parts of the gospel story "were easily distinguishable from the worthless—as distinguishable as diamonds in a dunghill." This was, he said, because the gospel writers were "ignorant, unlettered men" who propagated "superstitions, fanaticisms and fabrications."[1]

Obviously, the Jefferson Bible tells us a lot more about Thomas Jefferson than it does about the Lord Jesus. Miracles can't be so easily removed from the Jesus story, since they filled His ministry from beginning to end, and even His enemies couldn't—and didn't—deny His miracles. On the contrary, they claimed that He had done them aided by demonic powers. Unable to deny His mighty works, they sought to discredit them. The Jesus of Thomas Jefferson is not the Jesus of Scripture, and he isn't the Jesus of history. Why would a simple moral teacher so threaten the authorities that they needed to execute Him? How could a gentle moralist inspire His followers to launch a world-embracing movement that cost them their very lives? They certainly knew nothing of Thomas Jefferson's Jesus. The Jesus of Scripture and history is much more than a miracle-worker, but He is not less.

While the Bible of Jefferson is now a relic of history, the attempt to create a miracle-free Jesus continues. But the miracles of Jesus are not simply amazing displays of divine power; they are windows into His mission and ministry. During the course of this book, we will look at many of those miracles in some detail, but before we do, it's worth laying some groundwork by thinking about miracles in general, and Jesus's miracles in particular. For many moderns, the very idea of the miraculous is a vestige of a superstitious past. For others, the miracles of Jesus are intrusions to be removed, like bones from a fish, before the Jesus story can be digested by the enlightened mind.

As people who live in an increasingly secular society, we cannot avoid the questions related to the possibility and purpose of miracles. In this book, we will be studying the very pages Jefferson so carefully eliminated from his version of Jesus's life. The New Testament writers clearly did not regard miracles as dispensable. Rather, they were central to their understanding of Jesus, inextricably woven into His life and ministry. Consider, for example, these passages:

> And he went throughout all Galilee, teaching in their synagogues and proclaiming the gospel of the kingdom and healing every disease and every affliction among the people. So his fame spread throughout all Syria, and they brought him all the sick, those afflicted with various diseases and pains, those oppressed by demons, those having seizures, and paralytics, and he healed them. And great crowds followed him from Galilee and the Decapolis, and from Jerusalem and Judea, and from beyond the Jordan. (Matthew 4:23–25)

> Now when John heard in prison about the deeds of the Christ, he sent word by his disciples and said to him, "Are you the one who is to come, or shall we look for another?" And Jesus answered them, "Go and tell John what you hear

and see: the blind receive their sight and the lame walk, lepers are cleansed and the deaf hear, and the dead are raised up, and the poor have good news preached to them. And blessed is the one who is not offended by me." (Matthew 11:2–6)

Men of Israel, hear these words: Jesus of Nazareth, a man attested to you by God with mighty works and wonders and signs that God did through him in your midst, as you yourselves know—this Jesus, delivered up according to the definite plan and foreknowledge of God, you crucified and killed by the hands of lawless men. God raised him up, loosing the pangs of death, because it was not possible for him to be held by it. (Acts 2:22–24)

Basic Questions: The Nature and Possibility of Miracles

That the early Christians and the New Testament writers believed that Jesus had done miracles is beyond serious question. But what exactly are we talking about when we use the word *miracle*? In daily life, the popular use of the word *miracle* is very casual. When the American Olympic Hockey team unexpectedly defeated the Russians and then went on to win Olympic Gold in 1980, that victory became known as the "Miracle on Ice." When a passenger jet struck a flock of geese and was forced to make an emergency landing on the Hudson River, and did so without any loss of life, that event became known as the "Miracle on the Hudson." A friend unexpectedly recovers from a life-threatening accident or illness, and we hear her acclaimed as "a walking miracle." Or, which of us hasn't heard someone say, during the Christmas rush, "It was a miracle that I even found a parking place!"

All those events are certainly unexpected, and some even remarkably so. But do they merit the designation "miracle" in a biblical sense? Actually, the New Testament, in the original Greek, uses several words to describe what we've come to think of as miracles: an event that shows divine power (*dynamis*); a "wonder" (*teras*) producing amazement; a "sign" (*semeion*) pointing to something; or, most simply, Jesus often speaks of his "works" (*ergon*). It is entirely appropriate to see all of these as miracles, but we need to consider carefully what we are talking about.

It is common to speak of a miracle as "a violation of nature." Common as that definition may be, the word *violation* smuggles in the suggestion that such an act is, in some way, illegitimate, as if God himself is subject to the normal pattern of the creation that He brought into being. We can also use the term *miracle* to describe an extraordinary, unexpected event, a special grace that is an answer to prayer. More than once I have visited at a bedside, expecting soon to be conducting a funeral, only to witness, against all medical expectations, the person recovering to a significant degree. Some of these probably cross the border into the miraculous, and they are certainly reasons to praise and thank God, but they fall short of the unmistakable miracles we encounter in the life of the Lord Jesus.

Miracles in the Bible are very diverse, but they have certain qualities in common. In essence, they are events for which all naturalistic explanations are finally inadequate. They are temporary, extraordinary exceptions to the usual course of nature, things that would never happen, and could never happen, were natural processes left on their own. Some, in fact, stand in direct contrast to natural explanation. Water never, on its own, becomes wine. Undeniably dead people do not return to life. These are actions of God himself, but they are not sudden intrusions by a God who is otherwise absent or remotely unconcerned about His universe. The God of Scripture is always at work, present and sustaining His creation. When He chooses to work in a unique way, He is neither more present than usual, nor violating one of His own rules.

All well and good, but are we just fooling ourselves? Can miracles even happen? Loud and insistent voices tell us that the answer is No! The "age of miracles" has passed, they say, driven away by Enlightenment rationality and scientific discovery.

On the one hand, we find some who loudly declare, "Miracles are impossible. Reason and science tell us so." It is a claim that found its earliest voice in the work of Baruch Spinoza in the eighteenth century. Spinoza insisted that natural laws are immutable and cannot be broken. More recent voices chime their agreement. For example, Alex Rosenberg informs us that "the mistake, as Hume showed so powerfully, was to think that there is any more to reality than the laws of nature that science discovers." Ironically, this assertion, one which he says he learned from the philosopher David Hume, is in itself scientifically unprovable.[2] The always self-confident Richard Dawkins simply dismisses any doubt: "Events that are commonly called miracles are not supernatural, but part of a spectrum of more-or-less improbable natural events. A miracle, in other words, if it occurs at all, is a tremendous stroke of luck."[3]

There are important responses to such assertions. First, scientific investigation is premised on repeatable, reproducible experiments. But miracles, by their very nature, are neither repeatable nor reproducible. They are singularities, or anomalies, like the Big Bang. That does not mean that they are immune to investigation; it does mean that they are subject to a different kind of investigation than normal science can offer, a condition true to the investigation of all historical events. We should also observe that the "laws of nature" are not inviolable laws that exist independent of God. The Christian regards them as carefully made generalizations that describe the normal course of events in the known universe under the sustaining power and presence of God. He is not a prisoner of the nature He created. In that observation, we touch the central question. Naturalism assumes, without being able to prove it, that nature is all that exists. In the final analysis, the question is one of worldviews.

A second argument concerns itself not so much with the possibility of miracles as with their verifiability. These critics ask, "Miracles are unprovable, so where's the evidence?" It was the Scottish skeptic David Hume who gave classic expression to this challenge in the nineteenth century. In summary, Hume argued that because the evidence claimed for a miracle can never outweigh the certainty of the laws of nature, believing that a miracle has occurred will always be irrational, no matter how credible the witnesses appear. Everyone will always be in the position of having to accept what his own experience and the combined experience of humanity tell him can or cannot have happened. Coupled with this argument is the assertion that those who did claim to witness miracles in past centuries were largely ignorant and superstitious, living without the benefit of modern scientific knowledge. In fact, their very claims to have witnessed miracles reveal that they were credulous and easily deceived.

My summary is obviously a simplification of Hume's argument, and philosophers of all stripes have argued its validity for almost two centuries. This book does not allow us the space to enter into that debate in detail, nor is that its purpose. But several observations are in order. First, Hume's argument is ultimately circular: he assumes what he seeks to prove, that we live in a closed naturalistic system, into which no supernatural entities can enter. Furthermore, since by their very nature, miracles are not reproducible, repeatable, or predictable, there can be no "credible" witnesses by Hume's definition. Yet massive and persuasive evidence does exist for the most significant of miracles, the resurrection of the Lord Jesus from the dead.[4] It is also true that while ancient peoples did not know all that we now know about the way the world works, they knew more than enough to recognize some events as miraculous when they occurred. They knew that water does not become wine, that withered hands do not instantaneously become whole and functional, and that dead people, executed under the most gruesome and thorough conditions, remain dead.

Christians believe that because God exists as Lord of creation, miracles are both possible and actual. The possibility of miracles is inextricably bound up with the existence of God, and there are compelling reasons to believe in His existence. Moreover, we believe that the true God is not the remote and uninvolved god of deism, but the God who is active in history and who has revealed himself personally. God constantly upholds and sustains every part of creation. He does that in ways we've labeled "the laws of nature." But, on some occasions, for reasons that belong to Him alone, He chooses to change His normal pattern, which results in a miracle.

Supremely, God himself stooped to enter human history in the person of the God-man, the Lord Jesus. By His resurrection, a God-sized hole was torn into history. The credibility of the resurrection of the Lord Jesus is the fulcrum on which belief in miracles rests. In the light of the resurrection, the accounts of His miracles fit coherently, and on the basis of His authority, the miracle stories of the entire Bible gain credence. If He believed in them, so should we.

It must be said that belief in the reality of miracles is not a call to gullibility. Deception, naiveté, superstition, and ignorance are all part of the human experience. We should be skeptical of claims to miracles, since they are, by their very nature, rare and unpredictable. Too often, sincere Christians baptize dubious or exotic claims with credibility. To insist on the possibility of miracles is not to assert that all claims must simply be accepted. Christian faith is not belief without proof, but trust that rests on sufficient and credible evidence.

Marks of Majesty: The Miracles of Jesus

The miracles of Jesus are marks of His majesty and revealers of His person. The New Testament records at least thirty-five specific miracles performed by the Lord Jesus, most of them recorded in more than one gospel. As well, various passages allude to numerous other miracles performed in His ministry. As one of His closest followers, the apostle John notes, in the last verse of his gospel, "Now there are also many other things that Jesus did. Were every one of them to be written, I suppose that the world itself could not contain the books that would be written" (John 21:25). Broadly speaking, these miracles fall into three categories. Some are nature miracles, such as stilling a storm, multiplying loaves and fishes, and changing water into wine. Others are healing miracles—giving sight to the blind, hearing to the deaf, speech to the mute, movement to the paralyzed, and so forth. The third category is exorcism, or the expulsion of demonic beings from oppressed and victimized people. Combined, these miracles bear witness to the authority of King Jesus over the realms of nature, of human suffering, and of supernatural beings. As New Testament scholar Paul Barnett observes,

> The miracles of Jesus were always within the bounds of nature and not "contrary" to nature's patterns, that is, freakish or bizarre like the "signs" and "portents" that the Jews sought. His miracles were restrained, done for the good of those in need and not as spectacles in the manner of magicians. They served to point to Jesus as at one with the Creator in achieving His beneficent, end-time purposes on earth. In the miracles of Jesus the kingdom of God was present among them as the Son of Man went about doing good.[5]

The miraculous touches the life of the Lord Jesus in another way. The greatest miracle of all is not what He did, but who He is—God incarnate. In the words of C. S. Lewis, "The central miracle asserted by Christians is the Incarnation. They say that God became man. Every other miracle prepares for this, asserts this or results from this."[6] Because this is the case, miracles surrounded the earthly life of our Lord Jesus—His virgin conception, the angelic appearances, the heavenly signs witnessed by the magi and the shepherds, the descending dove at His baptism, His transfiguration appearance with Moses and Elijah, His resurrection, and His ascension back to heavenly glory. These were not miracles so much done by Jesus (although as God the Son He was, in some sense, their agent) but done to Him. His life was bathed in the supernatural, even as He had emptied himself of His divine glory (Philippians 2:7). That is an aspect of the miracles of Jesus that we will not be exploring in this book, although we must never forget it.

Our direct evidence of the miracles of Jesus comes from accounts in the Gospels, accounts of those who were either eyewitnesses or acquainted with eyewitnesses. But there are others who bear witness as well, some of them very reluctantly. For example, the Jewish leaders could not deny Jesus's amazing deeds, so they chose to attribute them to Satan: "The Pharisees said, 'He casts out demons by the prince of demons'" (Matthew 9:34); they asserted, "It is only by Beelzebul, the prince of demons, that this man casts out demons" (Matthew 12:24). For centuries, that claim would echo among the rabbis. The Jewish historian Josephus, writing in the last decade of the first century and with no personal reason to attribute miracles to Jesus, had He done none, writes, "At this time, there appeared Jesus, a wise man. He was a doer of startling deeds, a teacher of people who receive the truth with pleasure."[7] The Babylonian Talmud recounts a rabbinic tradition about Jesus:

"It has been taught on the eve of the Passover Jesus was hanged. For forty days before the execution took place, a herald went forth and cried, 'He is going forth to be stoned because he has practiced sorcery' (*b. Sanh. 43a*)."[8] One of early Christianity's staunchest critics, the Greek philosopher Celsus, was forced to acknowledge Jesus's miraculous powers, contending that because of His magical powers "he gave himself the title of God."[9]

There can be little doubt that even those most opposed to the Christian message could not deny that Jesus had a reputation as a successful miracle worker. They had, as Graham Twelftree observes, "no vested reason for portraying Jesus as a miracle worker if in fact he was not."[10] And even the most skeptical of modern scholars find themselves forced to acknowledge that people who encountered Jesus believed He did remarkable deeds. So, as Marcus Borg observes, "Despite the difficulty that miracles pose for the modern mind, on historical grounds it is virtually indisputable that Jesus was a healer and exorcist."[11] The skeptical Bart Ehrman acknowledges, "Whatever you think about the philosophical possibility of miracles of healing, it's clear that Jesus was widely reputed to have done them."[12]

Whether we are reading the gospel accounts or listening to the few voices that have been recorded by secular history, the conclusion is the same. The noted New Testament scholar N. T. Wright summarizes it well:

We must be clear that Jesus's contemporaries, both those who became his followers and those who were determined not to become his followers, certainly regarded him as possessed of remarkable powers. The church did not invent the charge that Jesus was in league with Beelzebub; but charges like that are not advanced unless they are needed as an explanation for some quite remarkable phenomena.[13]

More Than Marvels: The Meaning of Jesus's Miracles

As we prepare to make our way into the miracles of the Lord Jesus, it is helpful to direct our thinking to the meaning of Jesus's miracles. As we have said, they were acts of power, but they were far more than that.

While they were often awe-inspiring, His miracles were not spectacular feats designed to mesmerize the masses. In fact, one of Satan's temptations was for Jesus to perform just such a feat—to cast himself down from the pinnacle of the temple to call forth an angelic rescue (Matthew 4:5–8). Such an act might have aroused mass public enthusiasm, but it was not the Father's way. Jesus didn't relocate mountains, redirect rivers, or repel the Roman occupiers of Israel. Nor did He perform public relations stunts, as His unbelieving brothers suggested He do at the Feast of Tabernacles in Jerusalem (John 7:3–5).

He also refused to do miracles when the Jewish leaders demanded He do so (Matthew 12:38–39), obviously rejecting the opportunity to publicly discredit them. Even when He did perform majestic healings or exorcisms, He often commanded those He had healed not to tell others (Matthew 8:1–4; 9:27–31; 12:15–16). Never once did He say, as a modern television pitchman might, "Now, watch this!" His miracles lacked all the pageantry, grandstanding, manipulation, and greed of a showman.

Jesus's miracles were also not random acts of kindness, scattered haphazardly across the spectrum of human need. Although we are not always given an explanation, His miracles have a purpose beyond mere kindness. He had the power to heal anyone, anywhere, anytime. But He didn't. His miracles have purposes linked to His mission and His message. As we will see, His miracles are full of significance.

First, *Jesus's miracles are glimpses of His glory, revelations of His person.* John explicitly tells us, after describing Jesus's first miracle (which we will consider in the next chapter), that when He turned water into wine, He "manifested his glory" (John 2:11). Jesus insisted that the "works" He did revealed His unique relationship to the Father (John 5:36; 10:25; 14:11), and that to reject the witness of those works was to hate the Son, as well as the Father (John 15:22–24).

Second, *Jesus's miracles authenticate His authority and His message.* As Peter declared in Acts 2:22, Jesus is "a man attested to you by God with mighty works and wonders and signs that God did through him." His miracles were "the works that no one else did" (John 15:24). One of the striking features of Jesus's miracles is their display of ultimate personal authority. He did not recite healing formulae or engage in preliminary rituals. The Gospels do not even tell us that He prayed. Instead, He simply spoke, or touched, and it was done.

Third, *His miracles are foretastes of what will happen when the kingdom of Jesus is fully revealed.* In His person, the kingdom was already present, as He declared in Matthew 12:28: "But if it is by the Spirit of God that I cast out demons, then the kingdom of God has come upon you." The "if" in that statement presupposes that what follows is true: "Since I am casting out demons by the Spirit of God, then the kingdom of God is here."

In the person of Jesus, the kingdom of God was already present. But it was present only in preliminary form. When the Lord Jesus returns to establish His messianic kingdom in its fullness, as the prophets promised, He and His kingdom will be revealed in their full glory. Then, as Isaiah foresaw, "The eyes of the blind shall be opened, and the ears of the deaf unstopped; then shall the lame man leap like a deer, and the tongue of the mute sing for joy" (Isaiah 35:5–6). When Jesus performed such miracles at His first coming, He was giving us a foretaste of ultimate kingdom blessing, when the curse of man's sin will be removed and the Lord's glory will fill the earth as the waters cover the sea (Habakkuk 2:14). We await that day of completion, but in each miracle we are given a taste of it.

Fourth, *the Lord's miracles are a visible expression of His power and compassion.* The power is self-evident, and the compassion was visibly displayed as He touched the untouchable, included the excluded, brought joy to the bereaved, and released those bound by Satan.

Fifth, His miracles most obviously affected people's bodies, but *they also acted as parables of salvation.* The spiritually blind received sight, the grieving found peace, the hopeless found hope, the guilty found forgiveness, and the spiritually dead were restored to life.

It is to some of those miracles that we will now turn our attention.

—w—

A SIGN IN THE WINE

Weddings are special occasions, full of love, shared joys, and hopeful celebration. We come together as family and friends to share in a defining moment for people we love and care for. But, truth be told, weddings can also be times of great stress, runaway emotions, and isolated chaos, when fascinating things can happen. As a pastor, I've had the privilege of participating in hundreds over the years, but a few stand out for special and quite unique reasons.

I think of one wedding in which our entire family was deeply involved. It was years ago, at a time when a video recording of a wedding required the positioning of special lights. No one had informed us of this need, and during the rehearsal, we had carefully plotted the position of each person in the sizeable wedding party on a rather small platform. On the fateful day, the photographer arrived early and positioned his lights, which required shuffling some platform decorations. That would have been fine, except plugging in the lights in his chosen outlets blew a couple of fuses, leaving the auditorium in darkness and the electric organ silent as the guests began to arrive. After the panic that preceded finding a solution to that problem, the ceremony began with the processional accompanying each participant to their precise position on the platform. As I prayed a few moments later, I could smell something terrible. Looking around, I was startled to see that the bride's sister, one of her attendants, was standing too close to a repositioned candelabra, and her hair had caught fire! I immediately stopped what I was saying, pushed past my wife, who was serving as the matron of honor, and rushed to the startled woman to prevent a real disaster. It's not easy to return a ceremony to its appropriate dignity after that kind of excitement!

Then there was the wedding of a gregarious Scot, a local car dealer who loved to appear in his own television commercials. Magnificent in his ceremonial kilt, he was escorted into the church by a bagpiper resplendent in his own regalia. But then, at the critical moment, when he was to declare his vows, he was suddenly frozen speechless, almost unable to breathe. I had to lead him through the vows very deliberately, repeating almost every word, so he could declare his undying love.

A friend told me of a wedding he presided over in which the best man had been asked to read 1 John 4:18 at a special point in the service: "There is no fear in love, but perfect love casts out fear." Unfortunately, the man wasn't very familiar with the Bible, and didn't know the difference between 1 John and the gospel of John. When the time came, the pastor introduced the Scripture by saying he had asked the best man to read a passage that he thought was especially appropriate for the bride. And so the best man boldly read John 4:18: "For you have had five husbands, and the one you now have is not your husband." I hope my friend was stretching the truth with his story!

With all their foibles, weddings are great occasions. And it was at a small village wedding that the Lord Jesus chose to do the first of His mighty works. As we start our consideration of Jesus's miracles, we will begin where John did, at the miracle he records in the second chapter of his gospel.

The Setting: A Wedding Crisis in Cana

> On the third day there was a wedding at Cana in Galilee, and the mother of Jesus was there. Jesus also was invited to the wedding with his disciples. When the wine ran out, the mother of Jesus said to him, "They have no wine." And Jesus said to her, "Woman, what does this have to do with me? My hour has not yet come." His mother said to the servants, "Do whatever he tells you."
>
> Now there were six stone water jars there for the Jewish rites of purification, each holding twenty or thirty gallons. Jesus said to the servants, "Fill the jars with water." And they filled them up to the brim. And he said to them, "Now draw some out and take it to the master of the feast." So they took it. When the master of the feast tasted the water now become wine, and did not know where it came from (though the servants who had drawn the water knew), the master of the feast called the bridegroom and said to him, "Everyone serves the good wine first, and when people have drunk freely, then the poor wine. But you have kept the good wine until now." This, the first of his signs, Jesus did at Cana in Galilee, and manifested his glory. And his disciples believed in him. (John 2:1–11)

I can't help but wonder why, for His first public miracle, Jesus chose to turn water into wine. In the opening words of John's gospel, we are introduced to the truth of exactly who Jesus is. John describes Him as "the Word," the one who reveals the Father and who is himself God. "The Word was God . . . and without him was not any thing made that was made" (John 1:1, 3). I would expect the Word made flesh to launch His ministry with some grand spectacle in a major city. Today, would-be presidential candidates carefully craft their announcements for maximum effect. Surely the Messiah should begin His public career with something more impressive than providing the wine at a wedding in an obscure village! This is a setting and a miracle seemingly too small for who Jesus is and what He came to do.

But nothing that Jesus ever does is by accident. He always has a purpose, and as we look a little harder, this first miracle gives us a fascinating window into the central truth of His coming to live among us.

Cana was a small village in Galilee, about eight or nine miles from the Lord's home village of Nazareth. Nazareth itself was tiny, populated by only a few hundred people. Cana was larger, but still only a village. Both villages were home to poor people, eking out their living off the land or through minor building projects. These were enclaves not of the rich and powerful but of ordinary folk. Neither village was a place where significant events were supposed to take place or where important people were supposed to come from. As one of Jesus's first followers declared on hearing that Jesus was from Nazareth, "Can anything good come out of Nazareth?" (John 1:46). Interestingly, we discover at the end of the gospel that Nathaniel was from Cana (21:2). This clearly suggests that Cana was large and prosperous enough that its inhabitants could view Jesus's home village of Nazareth as a rural backwater in comparison.[1]

Weddings were special in such villages. They are always special in Jewish culture, but in such a place a wedding took on special meaning. These were people who lived very simple lives, but at a wedding they could pull out all the stops, inviting family, friends, and entire villages to share in their time of joy. The ordinary drabness and sameness of life gave way to feasting, celebration, and good fellowship. And weddings weren't simply a one-day event; they were usually a weeklong festival. Daily routines came to a standstill, as villagers seized the opportunity to share in the festivities.

We are given glimpses of first-century marriages throughout the New Testament. After a period of betrothal during which the couple was already spoken of as husband and wife, the great day would arrive. The day would begin with the groom making his way to his beloved's parents' home, where there would be a brief preliminary ceremony. Then he would return with his bride to his own home, or perhaps that of his parents, for the ceremony itself. Often there would be a great procession just after dark, with a group of young girls leading the groom and his bride through the early night, with their torches held high to light the way (the background for the Lord's parable in Matthew 25:1–13). It would be a magnificent spectacle as the procession wended its way through the streets, with the groom and bride being carried in a canopy, dressed like a king and a queen, accompanied by the sounds of musical instruments and singing.

Mary, the mother of Jesus, was among the guests. (Interestingly, John never refers to her by name in his gospel, but always as "the mother of Jesus.") It seems likely that she was either a relative or a close friend of the groom's parents. She lived only a few miles away, and the story suggests that she had an insider's knowledge of the wedding details and some degree of authority at the event. For example, she knew the significant catering problem, something unknown even to the feast's master of ceremonies. Jesus was also there, and with Him the disciples who had begun to gather around Him.

Unexpectedly, both Jesus and Mary found themselves caught up in a small yet significant crisis—the wine had run out! Jewish culture scorned drunkenness, but also celebrated wine. After all, the Old Testament had declared that "wine gladdens the heart of man" (Psalm 104:15), and the rabbis declared, "Without wine there is no joy." It represented life at its best, and for a host to run out of wine on such an occasion reflected badly on the family. A groom was to provide for his guests, and good hospitality was an almost sacred duty. So to run short of wine would be a social blunder that would be remembered in the village long after. This was no small matter in a culture of honor and shame. No one would die, but a family's reputation might suffer permanent harm.

The Sign: When Water Becomes Wine

How Mary learned of the problem we have no way of knowing. Armed with the secret, she rushed to Jesus and brought some of the servants with her. She simply announced the problem to her son: "They have no wine" (John 2:3). She obviously expected Jesus to do something, but what? A miracle? To this point Jesus had apparently not performed any miracles. The stories of Jesus as the boy doing miracles, like making clay pigeons and turning them into real birds, are the stuff of later Gnostic fantasies. The Bible mentions nothing of such things. Mary knew the true identity of Jesus, as no one else on earth did. She was also a widow, and He was her firstborn son. She had probably learned to lean on Jesus after the death of Joseph. Was she merely relying upon His proven resourcefulness? We have no way of knowing.

And the answer she received from her son surprises, even shocks, us: "Woman, what does this have to do with me? My hour has not yet come" (v. 4). The words grate on our ears—this hardly sounds like the way a respectful son addresses his mother, especially a sinless son. Why "woman" instead of "mother"? In our usage, "woman" used in this way would be heard as dismissive and disrespectful. But in the gospel of John, the Lord Jesus customarily uses this word to address women, always with courtesy, the equivalent of our "madam" or "ma'am." See, for example, Jesus's interactions with the Samaritan woman (4:21) and the woman taken in adultery (8:10). It is also the term the Lord will use to address His grieving mother from the cross, when in love He put her under the protective care of the apostle John. We read, "When Jesus saw his mother and the disciple whom he loved standing nearby, he said to his mother, 'Woman, behold, your son!' Then he said to the disciple, 'Behold your mother!'" (John 19:26–27). He was clearly not being dismissive or disrespectful, but concerned and protective. Respectful as Jesus's use of "woman" might be, it cannot be denied that it is distancing—hardly the way a Jewish man would ordinarily talk to his mother.

The next words also sound like a rebuke, albeit a gentle one, to our modern ears: "What does this have to do with me?" is actually "What business is that of ours?" or perhaps "Why are you meddling in this?" Mary had felt the freedom to assume that she, as his mother, had a right to include Jesus in such matters, as she desired. But He declared, "My hour has not yet come" (2:4). In the gospel of John, "the hour" or "my hour" is frequently used by Jesus to refer to His death on the cross, and His exaltation through it. Mary had no way of knowing what that "hour" involved, but the Lord knew that once He began to reveal His true identity and mission on the public stage, events would begin to unfold that would lead inexorably to His crucifixion. As Craig Keener observes, "His mother does not understand what this sign will cost Jesus: it starts Him on the road to His hour, the cross."[2]

So, in this abrupt response to His mother, the Lord was indicating that a turning point had been reached. Jesus would always be His mother's respectful son, but His life's mission was under the direction of His heavenly Father, not His earthly mother. She was, probably unintentionally, presuming inappropriately upon her relationship to Him. He was submissive to the Father, not to her.

I suspect that most of this didn't register with Mary. All she knew was that Jesus could do something about the wine problem, and thus prevent shame from falling upon the groom and his family. So she turned to the servants, whom she has commandeered for the occasion, with the simple directive: "Do whatever he tells you" (v. 5). She may have heard a gentle rebuke from Jesus; she hadn't heard a clear refusal. She had no idea what He might do, but she was confident He would do something!

John abruptly shifts our attention to part of the furniture at the banquet site: "six stone water jars . . . , each holding twenty or thirty gallons." These weren't ordinary water pots, providing water to drink. Stone jars of this size were both expensive and religiously significant, reserved for Jewish rites of purification. They were specifically intended for the ceremonial washings rabbis required before one could righteously participate in a meal, a requirement of tradition later to become a bone of contention between Jesus and the religious leaders (Matthew 15:1–19; Mark 7:1–23). The jars were made of stone, because stone would not become ceremonially unclean after being used. In rabbinical thought, clay pots would carry the contamination, and would therefore need to be destroyed after a single use. The purpose of such washing was not hygiene, but ceremonial cleanness. Therefore, they could contain only water, unmixed with any other beverage.

It was not accidental or incidental that Jesus chose these jars as the instrument of His miracle. They represented the religious ritualism that had come to dominate the Judaism of His time, and which He had come to confront. There were other sources of water present, and other containers. After all, the servants would have had those containers to fill these immovable stone pots. And filling them was no small matter. It would require numerous trips to a local water source to fill them completely. So, clearly Jesus was using these ceremonial pots not for practical reasons but for symbolic ones.

The method Jesus used was also deliberate. He could have commanded the servants to empty the pots before refilling them, to spill out all the water on the ground. That would have drawn everyone's attention. He could then have miraculously filled the empty jars with fine wine, a sensational miracle that no one could ignore. Instead, Jesus had them fill the pots to the brim. They were now completely filled with water, and not a small amount of water, but 120 to 150 gallons of it!

Jesus did no more. There was no loud word commanding the water to become wine, no public prayer to His Father, no ritual action, no loud shouts drawing attention to himself. He simply commanded the servants to draw out "water" from the pots and take the product to the master of the feast, a combination master of ceremonies and manager of arrangements. I cannot help but imagine the consternation and amazement of the servants, who had personally filled the pots with water, when they ladled out the contents and discovered that it was no longer water! One hundred and twenty gallons of water had amazingly and instantaneously become 120 gallons of wine—so much wine!

The master of the feast, oblivious to what had happened, now became an unintentional authenticator of the miracle. He perhaps recognized that an impending social error had been prevented and was glad to learn it had somehow been averted. With a loud voice, he rose to celebrate his hosts: "Everyone serves the good wine first, and when people have drunk freely, then the poor wine. But you have kept the good wine until now" (John 2:10). The strategy he refers to is an obvious one. The palate loses its sensitivity over time, so serve the good stuff first and the "Two-Buck Chuck" later. But the wine created by Jesus was not just any wine; it was the best of wines. By the Lord's power, looming shame had been turned into a triumphant badge of honor!

How many of the attendees at the wedding feast understood what had just happened? How many shared the wonder of the servants as they tried to explain this sudden abundance of wine? We are not told. But Mary knew, and so did the Lord's disciples. They had witnessed "the first of his signs" (v. 11). A veil had been removed for a moment, and they had briefly glimpsed the glory of the Lord Jesus, "glory as of the only Son from the Father, full of grace and truth" (1:14). And, having seen it, "his disciples believed in him" (2:11). They yet had long miles to travel on the road of faith, but they were well on the way to believing that "Jesus is the Christ, the Son of God," and that by believing they would "have life in his name" (20:31).

The Significance: Jesus, the Glory of God

John chose his words carefully. What he describes is clearly a miracle, an act of God for which there is no natural explanation. Water, over time, may stagnate or evaporate, but it will not, and cannot, become wine. But this was more than an act of power, unexplainable by the laws of nature. It was a *sign*—a word that John will use seventeen times in his gospel. A sign points to something or someone greater than itself. A sign is more than a supernatural display of power or an impressive spectacle. It is a teaching tool, more important for what it reveals than for what it is, in and of itself. Jesus didn't do what He did to satisfy thirsty guests or critical skeptics; He did it to reveal himself to those with eyes to see.

This first of His signs is *a sign of the Lord's person*. It "manifested his glory," as John states (2:11). At a minimum, this miracle shows that God is powerfully at work in the person of Jesus. As Nicodemus will declare, "Rabbi, we know that you are a teacher come from God, for no one can do these signs that you do unless God is with him" (3:2). But the disciples will come to recognize that Jesus not only has glory *from* God, He also possesses the glory *of* God himself. The gospel will end with Thomas on his face before the risen Christ, declaring, "My Lord and my God" (20:28). From this first miracle, it is evident that God is present. The sign of the wine isn't about weddings, but about the One who has the very power of creation, transforming water into wine.

So this is a miracle about the glory of Jesus. And yet, evident as that glory is, it is a veiled glory. This was a spectacular miracle done in the most unspectacular of ways. Most of the guests tasted and enjoyed the wine but missed the message.

This sign is also *a sign of the Lord's purpose*. It was no accident that He chose water pots that symbolized religious ritual and externalism to be the platform of this first miracle. Water can cleanse the external, but it can never cleanse the heart or satisfy the soul. Jesus was in effect announcing that He had come to replace the water of religion with the wine of His new life, His transforming presence. Wine is a symbol of joy and celebration, but it is also a symbol of suffering. One of the last things He did with His disciples was to take a cup of wine and fill it with new meaning: "This is my blood of the covenant, which is poured out for many for the forgiveness of sins" (Matthew 26:28).

Turning water into wine is also *a sign of the Lord's provision*. When He supplies, He does not do so sparingly or simply to meet the minimum required—120 to 150 gallons is a lot of wine. Some calculate it to amount to 2,400 servings! Since it is unlikely the wedding guests present could have imbibed that much, some suggest that the abundance was to give lasting proof of the miracle. The leftover wine in the stone pots would have provided tangible evidence that what had happened was not some kind of trick. Others suggest that the miracle bears witness to the abundance and overflow of God's grace in Christ. It is certainly evidence that He brings with Him fullness of joy, and points to the fact that while the world serves the best up front, the Lord Jesus always saves the best for last.

One final observation: this miracle is *a sign of the Lord's grace.* He did what He did quietly, so that not everyone knew what had happened or who had done it. He did what He did graciously. The groom did nothing to deserve this blessing. It was given on the basis of his need, not his merit. As a result, potential embarrassment was turned into excitement. The groom wasn't just spared shame, he was turned into a kind of social hero for doing the unexpected by providing the best wine last. The ordinary (a wedding) was turned into the extraordinary, a platform for the display of God's glory; and the obscure (the tiny village of Cana) was turned into a town we still remember two thousand years later. God's grace flows to the humble, and this miracle declares to us that our needs don't have to be urgent or extreme to be of concern to Him. He is the Lord of the little things and the little places, as well as the big things and the big places.

How many wedding guests enjoyed the wine but missed the sign? How many saw the bride and groom but missed the Lord? The servants saw a sign of His power and must have been impressed. But what then? The disciples saw beyond the sign to His glory. They believed in Him and followed Him. What about you?

T W O

—m—

SUPREME AUTHORITY

My father-in-law was brought up on the coast of Wales, in a little village called New Quay. It was a town that sent most of its young men to a life on the seas. And so, at the age of fourteen, a few years after the end of World War I, Mr. Jones was sent off to begin his maritime career, the fourth of his brothers to do so. It wasn't to be. He hated life at sea, and through God's remarkable providence, he jumped ship in the United States to seek his prodigal father in Canada. He found him, but what he found disappointed him profoundly—his father had made a home in Canada with another woman, while his wife and children remained in Wales. But, by God's grace, that disillusioning experience led him on a path that brought him to his heavenly Father. He began a lifelong adventure of walking by faith in the Lord Jesus, which impacted many lives, including—through his remarkable daughter—mine.

But his brothers remained at sea, three of them becoming ship captains, while his brother-in-law became one of the highest officials in the British Merchant Marine. As a result, early in 1953, an official-looking embossed envelope arrived at the home of Captain Alwyn Davies and his wife, bearing the royal seal and sent from Buckingham Palace. Opening it, they were thrilled and amazed to read the following:

> We greet you well. Whereas we have appointed the second day of June, 1953, for the solemnity of our coronation, these are therefore to will and command, all excuses set apart, that you make your attendance upon us, at the time above mentioned, there to do and to perform such services as will be required of you.

Captain and Mrs. Davies were being honored with an invitation to attend the coronation of the woman who would go on to become the longest serving monarch on the throne of Great Britain, Queen Elizabeth II. For a family of very humble roots, this was an enormous honor, in which my wife's extended family loves to bask. But it was hardly an invitation! "These are therefore to will and command, all excuses set apart" doesn't really give many options. Queen Elizabeth may only be a constitutional monarch, but when she speaks, her "subjects" respond appropriately. The words of a king or queen have power. How much more the words of the King of kings and Lord of lords!

As we have seen, when John introduced the ministry of the Lord Jesus, he began with an event at a humble village wedding celebration. There Jesus performed an act of creation, transforming water into the best of wine, and in so doing, "manifested his glory" (John 2:11). John has already spoken of Jesus's unique glory in John 1:14, declaring that "the Word became flesh and dwelt among us, and we have seen his glory, glory as of the only Son from the Father, full of grace and truth." John's design is to direct our attention beyond the miracle to the greatest miracle of all—not what Jesus did, but who He is: the God-man. The signs are about *Jesus's glory.*

When Jesus Speaks, God's Voice Is Heard

When Mark begins his account of Jesus's public ministry, he doesn't begin in the celebratory environment of a wedding feast, but rather in the quiet solemnity of a Sabbath synagogue service. Capernaum was a significantly larger town than Cana, and it was to became the Lord's base of operations for His Galilean ministry. As he begins to recount this singular day in the Lord's life, it is *Jesus's authority* that captures Mark's attention. It is the authority of a king, but not that of merely a human king. When Jesus speaks, not only is truth heard but also demons submit and diseases flee. So, in this chapter, we join Mark as he describes a remarkable day on which the supreme authority of Jesus is on full display.

> And they went into Capernaum, and immediately on the Sabbath he entered the synagogue and was teaching. And they were astonished at his teaching, for he taught them as one who had authority, and not as the scribes. (Mark 1:21–22)

Capernaum was a lakeside town on the northern shore of the (misleadingly named) Sea of Galilee, about twenty-five miles from Jesus's hometown of Nazareth. Featuring an extensive harbor and strategically located on a major trade route, it had a customs post and a detachment of Roman soldiers. A city of about ten thousand, it was the hometown of a number of the men Jesus had called to be His disciples, including Peter, Andrew, James, John, and Matthew, some of whom had been with Him at the wedding in Cana.

Jesus was an observant Jew, and He could regularly be found in a synagogue on the Sabbath. So it was on this day. Sabbath services followed a prescribed order of elements, including the recitation of various prayers and readings from the Torah and the Prophets. This was followed by a sermon on the Scripture, and great freedom was given to any man present to choose a passage and to speak. It was an opportunity the Lord Jesus used regularly (Matthew 4:23), and He did so on this occasion. Mark gives us no details of either the Scripture He read or the content of His message, although He has already described its essence: "Jesus came into Galilee, proclaiming the gospel of God, and saying, 'The time is fulfilled, and the kingdom of God is at hand; repent and believe in the gospel'" (Mark 1:14–15). In a postmodern world that elevates feelings, relativizes truth, and mocks the power of words, it is very important to recognize that teaching was central to the life and mission of the Lord Jesus.

The impact was electric: "They were astonished at his teaching, for he taught them as one who had authority, and not as the scribes" (v. 22). The scribes were the respected teachers of the day, the experts in Torah and tradition. They had great popular prestige for their position and their learning. They viewed their task as declaring, protecting, and explaining "the tradition of the elders" (Mark 7:3, 5). To that end, they leaned heavily on the insights and explanations of the great rabbis of the past, and their messages were full of verbal quotation marks and footnotes ("As Rabbi Nathan said, . . ."). They were not interested in innovation. Their authority was a derived authority.

In stark contrast, Jesus's teaching was fresh, personal, and persuasive. His message was both powerful and penetrating. At the same time, it was authoritative, conveying an undeniable ring of truth, a deep resonance between His words and reality itself. Those present sensed innately that He was not merely speaking *about* God; He was speaking *from* Him and *for* Him. His words were loaded with life and could neither be ignored nor forgotten. This wasn't the authority of human tradition or skilled rhetoric. This was inherent authority, coming from God himself. No wonder they were astonished at His teaching—they had not heard anything like this from anyone like Him before. So the first kind of authority Jesus displayed is *His authority to teach.* Sadly, however, astonishment at His authority is not the same thing as submission to His authority. It is one thing to be impressed by Jesus, but quite another to entrust oneself to Him.

When Jesus Commands, Demons Must Submit

> And immediately there was in their synagogue a man with an unclean spirit. And he cried out, "What have you to do with us, Jesus of Nazareth? Have you come to destroy us? I know who you are—the Holy One of God." But Jesus rebuked him, saying, "Be silent, and come out of him!" And the unclean spirit, convulsing him and crying out with a loud voice, came out of him. And they were all amazed, so that they questioned among themselves, saying, "What is this? A new teaching with authority! He commands even the unclean spirits, and they obey him." And at once his fame spread everywhere throughout all the surrounding region of Galilee. (Mark 1:23–28)

How many times had that man sat in such a service, quietly participating, with no unusual effects? But not this time! In the presence of the Son of God, the man under the influence of an unclean spirit suddenly felt a demonic being overwhelming him until he could be silent no more: "What have you to do with us, Jesus of Nazareth?" (v. 24). I imagine his shriek echoed off the stone walls of the synagogue. Almost certainly, nothing like this had ever happened in that synagogue.

Earlier in his gospel, Mark described how Satan had attempted to seduce Jesus away from His God-appointed mission through a series of temptations (Mark 1:12–13). His temptations had been thwarted by Jesus's submission to the Word of His Father, but the Evil One had not ceased his attempt to subvert or discredit the King. This becomes the first in a series of numerous encounters between Jesus and Satan's envoys. It should not surprise us that Satan and his demons should be especially active in opposition to the presence of their hated enemy. Nor should it surprise us that Jesus continually acted to liberate Satan's victims from his control. After all, as John tells us, "The reason the Son of God appeared was to destroy the works of the devil" (1 John 3:8).

Truth be told, talk of Satan and demons makes many of us uncomfortable, plunging some of us into deep skepticism. How can educated, informed people believe in a pathetic relic of ancient superstition? Surprisingly, despite the mockery of those who regard such beliefs as clearly absurd, a majority of American adults believe in both the existence and activity of Satan and demons.[1] Of course, the truth of demonology can't be established by opinion polls. For the Christian, the teachings of the Lord Jesus and the Word of God remain decisive. As well, God's Word has no room for the false and superstitious ideas that abound concerning the powers of darkness.

There is, however, a curious schizophrenia in our modern culture. Increasingly, we hear the mantra, "I'm spiritual, but not religious." But that "spirituality" turns out to be a curious and dangerous mixture. Our colleges and universities are witnessing a dramatic increase in people interested in modern witchcraft and pagan spiritualities, while pantheistic beliefs have become more mainstream. Furthermore:

> More than half of young adults in the U.S. believe astrology is a science, compared to less than 8% of the Chinese public. The psychic services industry—which includes astrology, aura reading, mediumship, tarot-card reading and palmistry, among other metaphysical services—grew 2%

between 2011 and 2016. It is now worth $2 billion annually, according to industry analyst firm IBIS World.[2]

It seems that the demonic realm isn't quite as foreign to modern life as we would like to believe. I suspect, however, there are perhaps fewer overt demon possessions in the Western world because Satan has found other tactics more fruitful.

In a later chapter, we will return to the subject of demon possession, but let me make some observations at this point, as we consider the Lord's miracle. First, *the powers of darkness are real*. The New Testament carefully distinguishes between demonic invasion of peoples' lives and other kinds of illness. This is not a simplistic explanation for otherwise unexplainable conditions or mental illnesses. Second, *the powers of darkness are evil*. They are not benign forces, and engaging such forces is not harmless. They represent an alien and evil authority. However they enter one's life, their ultimate effect is to attack, oppress, overpower, and destroy. Third, *the powers of darkness are present*. I have had several dramatic encounters with demonically oppressed people in North America. As well, the presence of dark spiritual forces is often more apparent in other parts of the world. Hearing the insights of trustworthy believers as I have ministered in such places has been eye-opening. Satan is no less active in our region. He just uses different means to achieve his nefarious ends.

The demonized man had previously been able to worship in the synagogue and not be disturbed. But the very presence of Jesus made everything different. In His presence, "all hell broke loose," and the demon, who had disabled his host, cried out in panic and alarm: "What have you to do with us, Jesus of Nazareth? Have you come to destroy us? I know who you are—the Holy One of God." That short outburst speaks volumes. The demon knew precisely who Jesus is—"the Holy One of God." He saw beyond the visible to the invisible, perceiving, as no human yet had, the true identity of Jesus, a pattern that is repeated throughout the Gospels. Demons had no trouble discerning the true identity of Jesus! At the same time, this demon feared Jesus's power. He knew that, should He choose to do so, Jesus could destroy him. Although there is a note of defiance in his words, their purpose was to disguise his fear. This was no battle of equals. The coming of Jesus was not good news for him. When the kingdoms of darkness and light collide, the outcome is not in doubt.

The Lord's response was simple and direct. He engaged in none of the elaborate incantations or magic rituals common to those who claimed the ability to exorcise demons. He did not even pray to His Father. He issued a single, crisp command: "Be silent [literally, "Be muzzled"], and come out of him!" (v. 25). Jesus simply would not accept the testimony of demons to His identity, no matter how true their words are (see Mark 1:34; 3:11–12). He also had no desire to inflame public emotions, in a context where someone claiming to be Messiah would have had immense political overtones. He did not come to be that kind of king!

The effect of His command was instantaneous and visible. With a final destructive surge of violence, the demon convulsed his victim, releasing a futile cry of rage, defiance, and frustration. He left behind a man now whole, sane, and free. One short demand from Jesus had set a captive free. This first exorcism also sets a pattern. When Jesus heals, the result is instantaneous and complete. He brings no partial healings, no deliverance by degrees, no half-way measures.[3]

If the teaching of Jesus had aroused wonder in the synagogue audience, how much more this remarkable event! If they had been astonished before, now they were astounded: "What is this? A new teaching with authority! He commands even the unclean spirits, and they obey him" (1:27). It is one thing to have remarkable authority in the realm of truth; it is quite another to have *remarkable authority over the powers of darkness*. But that is what Mark wants us to see: this Jesus has supreme authority in the sphere of truth *and* in the sphere of fallen spiritual beings. What is more, on the very same day, He was about to display His authority over the realm of sickness and death.

When Jesus Speaks, the Sick Are Made Well

And immediately he left the synagogue and entered the house of Simon and Andrew, with James and John. Now Simon's mother-in-law lay ill with a fever, and immediately they told him about her. And he came and took her by the hand and lifted her up, and the fever left her, and she began to serve them.

That evening at sundown they brought to him all who were sick or oppressed by demons. And the whole city was gathered together at the door. And he healed many who were sick with various diseases, and cast out many demons. And he would not permit the demons to speak, because they knew him.

And rising very early in the morning, while it was still dark, he departed and went out to a desolate place, and there he prayed. And Simon and those who were with him searched for him, and they found him and said to him, "Everyone is looking for you." And he said to them, "Let us go on to the next towns, that I may preach there also, for that is why I came out." And he went throughout all Galilee, preaching in their synagogues and casting out demons. (Mark 1:29–39)

Following the synagogue service, Jesus and three of His disciples made their way to Peter's home in Capernaum. If you visit Capernaum today, you will see the remains of a Byzantine church building said to be built on the site of Simon Peter's house, only a few yards from the ruins of a synagogue. The group arrived at Peter's home to enjoy a Sabbath lunch, only to find Peter's mother-in-law bedridden with a fever (Luke the physician calls it a "high fever" in Luke 4:38). We have no way of knowing the nature of her problem, but it was marshy around the lake, and some have suggested her ailment could have been malaria. Whatever the case, in a time before antibiotics and pain relievers, such a fever could prove very serious. It is worth noting that this was a Sabbath day, and it was against Jewish tradition (but not against the Torah) to heal on the Sabbath, unless death was imminent. There is no suggestion that Peter's mother-in-law was at death's door. Were He a tradition-bound rigorist, Jesus could and should have waited until that evening, when the Sabbath ended.

He did no such thing. Having been told about her problem as soon as He entered the house, perhaps as a warning to keep His distance from her, He acted immediately. Ignoring legalistic concerns, "He came and took her by the hand and lifted her up, and the fever left her" (Mark 1:31). Without speaking a word, by the mere touch of His hand, He dismissed the woman's illness. She was instantly and completely well, and with a Jewish woman's famed determination, she immediately set out to take care of her guests. Anyone who's had a severe fever knows that it takes time to regain strength. But this woman was fully healed, and almost certainly determined to serve Jesus as a way of expressing her gratitude to Him.

Word had already spread through the town about the remarkable events in the synagogue that morning. Perhaps news also spread about the dramatic healing of Peter's mother-in-law. So, when evening came and Sabbath restrictions ended, crowds spontaneously began to throng to Peter's house, bringing "all who were sick or oppressed by demons" (v. 32). Nothing had been planned or programmed. It seems these people were drawn by a mixture of astonishment, desperation, and hope. Mark gives us no details. He simply says that Jesus "healed many who were sick with various diseases, and cast out many demons" (v. 34). It is important to notice the distinction between the two categories. They did not attribute all illnesses to demons, nor was Jesus's power limited to certain kinds of physical problems. Whether their needs were in the realm of the physical or the spiritual, Jesus was able to resolve them all. And once again He silenced the demons, refusing to receive even grudging testimony from them. They were His enemies; He would not allow them to bear witness about Him.

What a remarkable day it had been! In the course of about twelve hours Jesus had revealed His sovereign authority in the realm of truth and over the realms of demonic powers and sickness. His miracle at the wedding in Cana had been somewhat muted. Only a few realized what had transpired. But now Jesus has manifested His divine authority in a very public way. His ministry has been fully launched.

But the episode that followed the next morning helps us to understand Jesus's priorities more clearly. Jesus had taken refuge in a remote place outside of town to spend time with His Father in prayer. When Peter and his companions finally found Him, they were full of excitement and anticipation: "Everyone is looking for you" (v. 37). Their meaning is that Jesus's acts of healing have aroused public interest to the point where, should He seize the opportunity, He could start a movement! With such miraculous and undeniable powers, He could sway crowds and create an unstoppable following. Success was just over the horizon. The disciples knew what He should do: strike while the iron is hot! Seize the moment!

The Lord's quiet response must have thoroughly confused them: "Let us go on to the next towns, that I may preach there also, for that is why I came out" (v. 38). His miracles were important, but they weren't most important. He had not come to engage in healing campaigns. His miracles were obviously done to meet needs but also, and more importantly, to authenticate His identity and the message He had been given by His Father. His disciples needed to learn that His ministry would not unfold in the way they expected. And in the course of time, they would come to realize that Jesus the miracle-worker and Jesus the teacher had an even greater mission. He is the Son of Man who came "not to be served but to serve, and to give his life as a ransom for many" (Mark 10:45)

We should observe that people were astonished and amazed at Jesus. But there is a great difference between being impressed by Him and entrusting oneself to Him. Many of those who were healed at His hand would never bow before Him in faith for their far greater need of healing from sin and rescue from the judgment to come. Experiencing Jesus's miracles is far less valuable than experiencing His salvation. Yet, too often we hear people craving the former and missing the latter.

We should also observe that this display of authority was only a foretaste of the day when the entire creation will bear witness to His authority, when "at the name of Jesus every knee [will] bow, in heaven and on earth and under the earth, and every tongue confess that Jesus Christ is Lord, to the glory of God the Father" (Philippians 2:10–11).

Toward the conclusion of Queen Elizabeth's coronation ceremony, at which my wife's relatives were privileged to be guests, the Archbishop of Canterbury turned to the assembled guests, the representatives of Elizabeth's scattered countries and realms in the Commonwealth, and asked: "I present to you her majesty Queen Elizabeth, your undoubted sovereign. Will you pay her homage?"

In a far more significant way, this day described in Mark 1 presents to us our undisputed Sovereign and Lord, King of all kings and Lord of all lords. Will you pay Him homage?

THREE

FISH STORIES

The story is told of a small-town family doctor who loved to fish and regularly boasted that he pulled in fish larger than anyone else in the area. No one openly challenged him, but if anyone seemed skeptical, he was quick to pull out his phone with pictures of his catches dangling from his fishing scales, showing their weight. One day, when he was busy fishing, a young man rushed up to him and said his wife had gone into labor and needed medical help immediately. The doctor grabbed his gear quickly, rushed to the woman's side, and soon delivered a healthy baby boy. The mother wanted to know how big her son was, and with no other device available, they decided to use the doctor's fishing scale. The boy weighed in at a healthy twenty-four pounds, six ounces!

Someone once raised the question, "Do all fishermen lie, or do only liars fish?" Another contended that "all fishermen were born honest, but they get over it." As one cynic declared, "Hunters lie in wait, while fishermen wait and lie." Remarkably, researchers have actually investigated the phenomenon, and one study concluded that the propensity for lies was directly related to the length of time between catches! So, as the maxim goes, "There's more to fishing than knowing how to tie a tie or cast a line. You also need to learn how to stretch the truth."

Rightly or wrongly, fishermen have a reputation for a rather ambivalent relationship with truth. As a result, fishing stories generally belong in the fiction section of the library. Nevertheless, despite their shady reputation, in this chapter we are going to look at two fish stories that involved miracles by the Lord Jesus. These stories are not just completely true, they were life-changing for those who experienced them firsthand. The two miracles are virtual twins, although one occurred close to the beginning of the Lord's public ministry, the second near the very end, His last recorded miracle before His return to His Father in heaven. Both involve fishing, and both were probably witnessed only by Jesus's disciples, many of whom were professional fishermen. In both of them, Peter is the major character. The display of Jesus's power on Lake Galilee, where these men had spent much of their lives as professional fishermen, left an indelible impression. The miracles clearly displayed the Lord's divine power; more importantly, they clarified the Lord's purpose for these men, a purpose that would redirect the entire course of their lives.

The First Fish Story: "I Will Make You Fishers of Men"
The first of the stories is recorded for us in Luke 5:1–11. Earlier, Jesus had encountered four of the disciples whom we know were fishermen—Peter, Andrew, James, and John, as they were casting their nets into the sea. They were already devoted to Jesus—they had been present at the miracle in Cana that we discussed in chapter 1. At that time He had called them to follow Him, an episode recorded in Matthew 4:18–21 and Mark 1:16–20. And so they had. But while they were followers of Jesus, they continued to be engaged in fishing. Now, in an event very similar to that first summons, and

yet clearly distinct, Jesus would call them to a complete change in their lifestyle, upending their plans for the future.

> On one occasion, while the crowd was pressing in on him to hear the word of God, he was standing by the lake of Gennesaret, and he saw two boats by the lake, but the fishermen had gone out of them and were washing their nets. Getting into one of the boats, which was Simon's, he asked him to put out a little from the land. And he sat down and taught the people from the boat. And when he had finished speaking, he said to Simon, "Put out into the deep and let down your nets for a catch." And Simon answered, "Master, we toiled all night and took nothing! But at your word I will let down the nets." And when they had done this, they enclosed a large number of fish, and their nets were breaking. They signaled to their partners in the other boat to come and help them. And they came and filled both the boats, so that they began to sink. But when Simon Peter saw it, he fell down at Jesus' knees, saying, "Depart from me, for I am a sinful man, O Lord." For he and all who were with him were astonished at the catch of fish that they had taken, and so also were James and John, sons of Zebedee, who were partners with Simon. And Jesus said to Simon, "Do not be afraid; from now on you will be catching men." And when they had brought their boats to land, they left everything and followed him. (Luke 5:1–11)

As we saw in the last chapter, the Lord had established the base of His ministry in Capernaum, on the shores of the Sea of Galilee, the lowest freshwater lake in the world. The lake was the primary source of fish for the Jewish people, and fishing was a major economic industry for the region. The lake itself is about 150 feet deep at its deepest point, and because of the structure of the lake bottom, the shallower northern end was a gathering spot for fish, especially in colder months.[1] We are told that the lake contained eighteen varieties of fish, ten of which were commercially desirable. The first-century Jewish historian Josephus, a resident of the area for lengthy periods, declares that "the lake contains species of fish different, both in taste and appearance, from those found elsewhere."[2]

Early one morning, Jesus made His way to the shores of Lake Galilee, near an area where He knew His disciples harbored their boats and stored their nets. Early though it was, crowds drawn by His teaching and miracles were already pressing in to hear His words. For a time He stood near the lakeshore, facing the crowds, with His back to the lake.[3]

At some point, the Lord chose a different method. He turned to His friends and disciples who were nearby, busily washing and perhaps mending their nets after a long night's fishing. This was standard and essential practice for commercial fishermen—nets needed to be washed and hung to dry, so they wouldn't rot and would be ready for the next outing. Fishing was their livelihood, their means of support for their families, not merely a hobby for people desiring a change of pace. These were tired men, longing for sleep, but when Jesus asked if He could use their boat, Peter quickly volunteered his. Sitting in a boat would give Jesus relief from the pressing crowds, and the lake would act as a natural acoustic, enabling His voice to carry more easily. Almost certainly Peter felt privileged to help the Lord in this way.

How long Jesus sat teaching the crowds, we are not told. Sitting wasn't just a matter of good practice in a boat; it was the posture Jewish rabbis regularly took when they taught. But all good things come to an end, and when the time came for His teaching to conclude, Jesus ended it in an unexpected way. Rather than asking Peter to return Him to shore, He issued a command: "Put out into the deep and let down your nets for a catch" (Luke 5:4). This was not a casual suggestion. It was a command—the guest was commandeering the boat! And it wasn't a small request. Putting out the nets would mean a lot of repeated work for His friends.

Nor was it, to any fisherman's mind, a reasonable request—it went against everything fishermen knew to be wise practice. This was not the time of day to cast nets. We should observe some things here. Fishing in Lake Galilee was hard work. As David Bivin notes, "The Sea of Galilee fishermen were tough. Their bodies were wet most of the time, even in winter, for it is during the winter that fishing is at its best on the Sea of Galilee. . . . The fisherman's work is also hard physically, entailing rowing to and fro from the fishing sites, hauling in heavy nets and lifting catches of fishes."[4] It wasn't only that the Lord was asking them to repeat hours of hard work. Fishing in Lake Galilee was best done at night because the fish could not see the strands of the net. If they weren't being trapped at night, they almost certainly wouldn't in broad daylight!

Peter, the professional fisherman, knew all this. And so he protested, "Master, we toiled all night and took nothing!" If they had failed at night, failure was all the more certain now. This was the wrong time. But Peter's respect for the Lord Jesus was too high for him to refuse His command: "But at your word I will let down the nets" (v. 5). So they pushed out into deeper water and let down the nets. This was no small task, and I wonder what kind of grumbling went on in their hearts, if not on their lips.

And then the impossible! They had no sooner set the nets than an avalanche of fish hit them. Frantically, they tried to pull in the nets but hundreds of pounds of fish were breaking their backs and tearing their nets. Urgently they summoned their fellow fishermen on the shore for help, and together they began to pull the nets into the boats. But now they had another problem—the boats themselves were beginning to sink under the load!

Peter was dumbfounded. Everything he knew from years of experience told him that what he was witnessing did not, and could not, happen. It was a miracle, one in the area of his supposed expertise. He turned from the greatest catch of his lifetime to fall at the feet of Jesus in the boat: "Depart from me, for I am a sinful man, O Lord" (v. 8). His physical posture of reverence was reflected in his words of address. Moments earlier he had addressed Jesus as "Master" (v. 5); now he fell before Him, addressing Him as "Lord." While the word often simply connotes a person of authority, here it has a profound significance. He is awestruck by a profound realization of who Jesus truly is, one greater than a mere human.

For Peter, deeper insight into the identity of Jesus came with a deeper understanding of himself. He saw himself as a sinful man, unworthy to be in the presence of Jesus. There is a strong similarity to the experience of Isaiah the prophet, recorded in Isaiah 6. He "saw the Lord sitting upon a throne, high and lifted up" (v. 1), as heavenly beings celebrated His holiness and glory. But Isaiah's response wasn't one of exhilaration; rather, it was fear and humiliation: "Woe is me! For I am lost; for I am a man of unclean lips, and I dwell in the midst of a people of unclean lips, for my eyes have seen the King, the LORD of hosts" (Isaiah 6:5). Like Isaiah before the throne of God, Peter's privilege of glimpsing the true nature of Christ was both awesome and awful, exposing his profound sinfulness and the Lord's transcendent holiness.

The Lord, however, did not reinforce Peter's sense of unworthiness. Instead, He extended grace: "Do not be afraid." It is remarkable how often these words appear in the Bible in the context of a person encountering the supernatural, whether God himself or an angel representing Him. For Peter, this was a word of grace, forgiveness, and acceptance. Sinful though he was, the one he recognizes as Lord accepts him. Indeed, the Savior both reassured and commissioned him: "Do not be afraid; from now on you will be catching men" (Luke 5:10). His future would now take an abrupt turn: he would not be engaged with dead fish, but with living people. Peter could have little idea, if any, what the Lord meant by "catching men," nor could he have imagined that the scope of that activity would take him across the Mediterranean Sea, not merely around Lake Galilee.

Peter may not have known the details of the Lord's plans for him, but he trusted Jesus enough that he was willing to walk away from the greatest catch of fish and into a new life with Jesus. I wonder how he explained this change of life focus to his wife! But perhaps she understood—after all, her mother had experienced the Lord's healing power. Peter's mother-in-law may have been his biggest cheerleader!

We too are called to follow the Lord Jesus and to join Him in the mission of "catching people." We may not have the special privileges or the unique calling that Peter had as an apostle. But what was true for Peter on that day long ago on Lake Galilee is also true for us: when we really begin to see Jesus as He is, everything else pales in comparison. We may not be called to walk away from our professions, but we will begin to see our jobs in a new light as we follow Him.

The Second Fish Story: "Feed My Sheep"

Remarkable as this first fish miracle was, it has a sequel at a very different time in the Lord's life. The previous miracle had taken place close to the beginning of His public ministry. The "repeat performance" came as one of the last experiences the disciples would have with the Lord Jesus, this time with the risen Christ. The account is found in John 21, and it's His last recorded earthly miracle.

> After this Jesus revealed himself again to the disciples by the Sea of Tiberias, and he revealed himself in this way. Simon

Peter, Thomas (called the Twin), Nathanael of Cana in Galilee, the sons of Zebedee, and two others of his disciples were together. Simon Peter said to them, "I am going fishing." They said to him, "We will go with you." They went out and got into the boat, but that night they caught nothing.

Just as day was breaking, Jesus stood on the shore; yet the disciples did not know that it was Jesus. Jesus said to them, "Children, do you have any fish?" They answered him, "No." He said to them, "Cast the net on the right side of the boat, and you will find some." So they cast it, and now they were not able to haul it in, because of the quantity of fish. That disciple whom Jesus loved therefore said to Peter, "It is the Lord!" When Simon Peter heard that it was the Lord, he put on his outer garment, for he was stripped for work, and threw himself into the sea. The other disciples came in the boat, dragging the net full of fish, for they were not far from the land, but about a hundred yards off.

When they got out on land, they saw a charcoal fire in place, with fish laid out on it, and bread. Jesus said to them, "Bring some of the fish that you have just caught." So Simon Peter went aboard and hauled the net ashore, full of large fish, 153 of them. And although there were so many, the net was not torn. Jesus said to them, "Come and have breakfast." Now none of the disciples dared ask him, "Who are you?" They knew it was the Lord. Jesus came and took the bread and gave it to them, and so with the fish. This was now the third time that Jesus was revealed to the disciples after he was raised from the dead.

When they had finished breakfast, Jesus said to Simon Peter, "Simon, son of John, do you love me more than these?" He said to him, "Yes, Lord; you know that I love you." He said to him, "Feed my lambs." He said to him a second time,

"Simon, son of John, do you love me?" He said to him, "Yes, Lord; you know that I love you." He said to him, "Tend my sheep." He said to him the third time, "Simon, son of John, do you love me?" Peter was grieved because he said to him the third time, "Do you love me?" and he said to him, "Lord, you know everything; you know that I love you." Jesus said to him, "Feed my sheep." (John 21:1–17)

The episode took place at least two weeks after the resurrection of the Lord Jesus. We don't have enough data to reconstruct events precisely, but we know that the disciples had remained in Jerusalem for at least that long. During that time the risen Lord had appeared to them numerous times, times that for Peter had been particularly significant. After all, he had denied and abandoned the Lord at the worst of times. And yet the risen Christ had sought him out, forgiven him, and restored him despite his abject failures.

On resurrection morning, the Lord had commanded His men to leave Jerusalem and to return to Galilee, where He promised to meet them (Matthew 28:10). So they did as He commanded. We are told nothing of their journey back to familiar territory, but we can imagine the mixture of emotions along the way. Leaving Jerusalem was hard: so many awful and awesome things, from crucifixion to resurrection, had occurred there. Galilee would have felt both familiar and strange at the same time. There were the comforts of home, reunions with family and friends, memories of times with Jesus. But nothing was the same. How could it be, when you had experienced a crucified, resurrected Lord! Family and friends were fine, but when would they see Him again?

One afternoon, during this waiting period, when seven of the disciples were together, Peter suddenly announced to the others that he was going to spend the night fishing. The others quickly agreed to join him. Some suppose that this was something more than a casual suggestion, that Peter was stating his intention to return to his old way of life. That hardly seems plausible, given what we know of the disciples' life-transforming encounters with Jesus. It is far more likely that, in light of the stupendous events they had encountered, as well as the intimidating threats and reprisals of the Jewish leadership, Peter just wanted to enjoy the familiar comforts of life on the lake. It may have been an impulsive decision, but being impulsive isn't the same as being rebellious. Perhaps Peter was growing impatient, anticipating what the Lord was going to do next. Who wouldn't? Any honest Christian must admit that waiting for the Lord can be a difficult assignment. We are often in a hurry, and He doesn't seem to be, at least by our schedule. Rather than fretting, perhaps Peter and the others just wanted to get away and unwind. Perhaps they could also make a little money on the side. After all, they still had families to support.

Whatever the reason, their fishing expedition turned into another long and frustrating night. As John, who was with them in the boat, recalls: "That night they caught nothing" (John 21:3).

As the gloom of night was beginning to lift and their time on the lake was drawing to a close, a lone figure appeared on the shore. Through the haze, He was visible, but too far away to recognize. And when He shouted at them, "Children, do you have any fish?" they didn't recognize His voice. The stranger barked back a suggestion: "Cast the net on the right side of the boat, and you will find some." When the Lord has issued His strange instructions at the first fish miracle, they had at least known who was speaking. This time, they had no idea who was speaking. And logic says that if they couldn't see Him, how could He possibly see fish lurking on one side of the boat rather than the other? I have no idea why they paid attention, why the career fishermen didn't scoff at the very idea, dismissing it as nonsensical. They knew the lake; why would they listen to an anonymous stranger?

But they did. And, implausibly, once again, the nets were attacked by an unprecedented abundance of fish. Even though these experienced fishermen did their best to haul in the loaded nets, the job was beyond their capacities. For John, all the alarm bells went off in his head. This was too familiar: "It is the Lord!" he told Peter (v. 7). Indeed it was. The amazing catch wasn't the product of an astonishing coincidence. It wasn't because, as the omniscient One, He knew the fish were there. No, they were there because He had caused them to be there—the One who shepherds the stars was shepherding those fish into His disciples' nets.

John's instant recognition was followed by Peter's immediate reaction. Wrapping his outer robe around him, he threw himself into the lake and wrestled his way through the waters to Jesus. Did he swim? Could he swim? I don't know, but I do know he raced to the Lord in joyous excitement. Remember that on the first occasion, he had fallen fearfully at Jesus's feet, conscious of his sins, and asking Jesus to depart. This time, as a forgiven sinner, he raced joyfully to his Lord, delighting at His presence. What a difference the cross and empty tomb had made!

That breakfast on the beach with Jesus as the host must have been very special. One of a Christian's great privileges is to enjoy fellowship with Him at the table where He is the host, where the meal isn't roasted fish, but bread and wine. As career fishermen, they were very careful to count the fish—153 in all. Few verses have spawned more speculation than the possible symbolism of that number. For the present, we'll resist the temptation.

For our purposes, it's important to note that this miracle story of fish ends very similarly to the first, with a commissioning of Peter for ministry. In the first case, the Lord called Peter to spend his life catching living people, not marketing dead fish. In this sequel, the risen Good Shepherd commissions Peter to feed and care for God's people, His lambs and sheep. This is a wonderful story in itself, but here our purpose is to keep our eyes on the big picture. The Lord called Peter to demonstrate his love by caring for the people He had suffered and died for.

Peter's love for the Lord was far from perfect, but it was real. Jesus knew that, but He wanted Peter to know that a primary way we show our love for Jesus is by loving what matters most to Him, the people who form His church, the people for whom He died. Peter's responsibility was a unique one; he was an apostle. But while that role was special, our responsibility is, at its core, the very same as his: *Love for the Lord is expressed by loving His people.*

It is no accident that the Lord's ministry was framed by very similar miracles—miracles that He used to reveal His person, power, and purpose. His power makes the impossible possible. His presence makes holiness visible, driving us to our knees in confession, humility, and reverential awe. His grace calls us to our feet in acceptance and forgiveness, inviting us to enjoy fellowship at His table. His command commissions us to new priorities, giving ourselves to His mission in the world. We may not be eyewitnesses of His fish-multiplying power, but we are recipients of His life-transforming grace. So His business must be our business and His purposes, our purposes.

The first fish miracle brought Peter to the Lord's feet in repentant, humble awe of His power. The second miracle brought Peter rushing to the Lord in joyful, grace-based gratitude and love. Each of these is an attitude we need to cultivate in our lives—worship and gratitude at the feet of our Savior. Both miracles also show us that when we obey the Lord's commands, He is faithful to supply the resources we will need. And they also help us understand that we are recipients of grace in order to be distributors of grace to all those the Lord sends our way.

FOUR

A PORTRAIT OF GRACE

In the first three centuries of Christian history, two devastating plagues swept through the Roman Empire: smallpox in 165 and an unknown disease in 251. The death tolls were appalling: one-third of the empire died during the first plague; and in the second, about five thousand people died every day in the city of Rome, while two-thirds of the population of Alexandria succumbed. The reasons are fairly obvious from a public health standpoint. As one scholar observes, "The Greco-Roman city was a pesthole of infectious disease,"[1] densely crammed as it was with people, and afflicted with unclean water, terribly inadequate sewage systems, murky darkness, and smoke-filled air.

The obvious solution was for the healthy to flee the infected city and spare themselves. Thousands did, abandoning the sick and dying to fend for themselves.

What is remarkable is how many of the early Christians responded differently. Rather than moving away from the cities, they moved toward them. Rather than saving themselves, they risked their lives to serve the needy. Dionysius, an early Christian leader in Alexandria, Egypt, describes the Christian response at the height of the plague:

> Most of our brother Christians showed unbounded love and loyalty, never sparing themselves and thinking only of one another. Heedless of danger, they took charge of the sick, attending to their every need and ministering to them in Christ, and with them departed this life serenely happy; for they were infected by others with the disease, drawing on themselves the sickness off their neighbors and cheerfully accepting their pains. Many, in nursing and curing others, transferred their death to themselves and died in their stead. . . . The best of our brothers lost their lives in this manner. . . . The pagans behaved in the very opposite way. At the first onset of the disease they pushed the sufferers away and fled from their dearest, throwing them into the roads before they were dead and treated unburied corpses as dirt, hoping thereby to avert the spread and contagion of the fatal disease.[2]

Where did those men and women learn to do that—to run toward the untouchables rather than away from them in fear, to risk danger rather than practice self-preservation? The answer is simple but incredibly challenging. They had seen it in the life of the Lord Jesus, and they were convinced that if they claimed to follow Him, they needed to do what He would have done. The coronavirus pandemic has given us a firsthand encounter with the dangers and difficulties induced by such an event. Ironically, our Christian love calls us to "socially distance" to protect the vulnerable, while their situation called for ordinary people to become frontline workers. But Christian love, in whatever form it takes, always follows the example of Jesus.

When we look at the miracles of the Lord Jesus, we need to do more than wonder at His power. We need to see His miracles as pictures of God's grace in action, ultimately pointing us to salvation in Christ. And we also need to see them as pointers to His purpose for our lives. Obviously, we do not possess His divine powers, but we do possess His indwelling Holy Spirit, and we are called, as Peter says, to "follow in his steps" (1 Peter 2:21), as we live as His kingdom agents in the world. The miracles we will consider in this chapter, described in Matthew 8, call us not just to open our eyes, but to open our hearts to a hurting world.

"If You Are Willing": Grace Touches the Untouchable

> When he came down from the mountain, great crowds followed him. And behold, a leper came to him and knelt before him, saying, "Lord, if you will, you can make me clean." And Jesus stretched out his hand and touched him, saying, "I will; be clean." And immediately his leprosy was cleansed. And Jesus said to him, "See that you say nothing to anyone, but go, show yourself to the priest and offer the gift that Moses commanded, for a proof to them." (Matthew 8:1–4)

Each of the gospel writers tells the story of Jesus in his own particular way, often giving us the same stories in a different pattern. For example, Mark follows the life of Jesus in a broadly chronological way. Matthew, on the other hand, arranges his material in a more topical fashion. This is particularly true in Matthew 8 and 9, where he clusters the miracles of Jesus, interspersed with the Lord's teaching about discipleship. His approach is thematic, rather than strictly chronological. Luke, for his part, combines the two approaches. Those differences are evident in the way each writer presents the two miracles we will consider in this chapter.[3]

We will consider these miracles primarily as Matthew recounts them. In Matthew 8 and 9, he records ten miracles of Jesus, which he groups into three clusters, the first two with three miracles, and the third with four. We will focus on two of the three in his first cluster, since we have, in fact, already considered the third of the three, the healing of Peter's mother-in-law. Each of these three reveals the Lord's compassion for those outside of the mainstream of Jewish society—a leper, a Gentile, and a woman.

Few conditions were as devastating in ancient Israel as leprosy. Luke, with his physician's eyes, describes the man who suddenly breaks into the crowds to kneel in desperation before Jesus as "full of leprosy" (Luke 5:12). In our modern world of medicine, with its precise diagnostics, *leprosy* is a term reserved for Hansen's disease, a heartbreaking condition that distorts and deforms by robbing its victims of the sensation of pain. As a result, the afflicted person can unknowingly inflict on himself terrible damage, since he or she lacks the signals that nerves are intended to send, warning of danger. Not being able to feel pain, in this case, is a terrible curse, not a blessing. However, the terms translated "leprosy" in our English Bibles could refer to a number of maladies that affect a person's skin. Prior to modern antibiotics, many of those diseases would be highly contagious and even deadly in their effect.

Leprosy, however, was far more than an ailment to be addressed with clinical detachment. There were layers upon layers of implications for a person with leprosy, touching every area of a victim's life.

Physically, he was hopeless. It was believed that it was as hard to heal leprosy as it was to raise the dead. In the whole of the Old Testament, we're told of only two people who were healed of leprosy: Miriam and Naaman (Numbers 12:10–16; 2 Kings 5:1–14).

Socially, he was isolated. The Old Testament established a rigorous system of isolation for lepers (see Leviticus 14:33–56), and as a result, leprosy meant living as an outcast, stigmatized by society. In practical terms, this man had lost contact with his family, his friends, his work, his home, and any kind of normalcy. In addition, the rabbis had layered on even more restrictions, designed to protect others. If a person was touched by a leper, he needed to follow a procedure of ceremonial cleansing. If clothing was touched by a leper, it was to be burned. If a pot or plate was used by a leper, it was to be shattered. No wonder it has been said that "a leper was a corpse haunting the edges of a community he could no longer enter."

But a leper's problems did not end there. *Emotionally, he was shamed.* Whenever anyone came close, he was required to sound the warning, "Unclean! Unclean!" Inevitably, people came to believe that lepers were getting what they deserved and would treat them not only with caution but also with contempt. After all, they may have reasoned, the Old Testament revealed that Miriam, Gehazi, and King Uzziah had each been struck with leprosy as a judgment for sin. As a result, *religiously, this man was excluded.* A leper was not allowed to approach a priest, enter the temple, or experience corporate worship in the temple or a synagogue. In every sphere of life, a leper was a social pariah, an outsider resigned to looking in but never being in.

So it was no small matter when this man came bursting through all those cultural barriers to fall at the feet of Jesus. Almost certainly, those close to Jesus shrank back in fear at the leper's closeness. He was supposed to stay at a distance, but he couldn't and wouldn't. News about Jesus had opened a window of hope. So, with enormous risk but very little to lose, he fell to his knees before Jesus in a posture of reverence, dependence, and petition. His were words of hope-filled faith: "Lord, if you will, you can make me clean" (Matthew 8:2).

The statement is remarkable. Clearly he knew he was addressing no ordinary man. His only question was about the Lord's willingness, not His ability. Was there a place in His heart for a leper? Jesus could heal him, but would He? The Gospels don't tell us if Jesus had healed lepers prior to this, but reports of Jesus's astonishing miracles must have reached this desperate man. Perhaps he had become convinced that Jesus was at least as powerful as Moses or Elisha, the only two people in the Old Testament connected to the healing of a leper.[4]

Instinctively, people would have drawn back from the near presence of a leper in fear and disgust. But Jesus defied the norms by immediately demonstrating His readiness with a simple touch. He didn't need to touch the man; He could have removed the leprosy with a direct word of command. Instead, He deliberately reached out to touch him, to show both the man and those observing His love and compassion. How long had it been since the man had been touched by a loving healthy hand? Jesus was bridging years of shame and stigma. Technically, touching the leper had made Jesus ceremonially unclean. But His touch didn't defile Him; it transformed the leper!

His touch of compassion was accompanied by a word of divine authority: "I will; be clean." With those simple words, the man was instantly, totally, and permanently changed. All traces of his disease vanished. Each of the gospel writers tells us the healing happened "immediately," so that we don't miss the point: Jesus's healings were immediate and complete.

Jesus's next words, however, strike us as somewhat strange: "See that you say nothing to anyone." What could that mean? After all, Jesus had performed this miracle in public, in the presence of numerous witnesses. It could hardly be kept secret. Most likely, the reason lies in another direction. The man had been fully and totally healed, and was physically a leper no longer. But his status as a leper wasn't just medical; it was also social and religious. He had been declared a leper by a priest's proclamation. That status could only be removed by a second priestly proclamation, a procedure laid out in Leviticus 14:1–32. A healed or recovered leper was to present himself to the priest, so that his healed condition could be verified, and was to offer a sacrifice as prescribed in the law. There must have been a tremendous temptation for this man to seek out his estranged family and friends, to celebrate with them his reentry into life. But Jesus counseled obedience to God's law. Such obedience would be "proof" not only of the completeness of the healing but also that Jesus, the One who touches and heals lepers, cared about the law of God.

Matthew doesn't tell us what followed, but Mark and Luke do. Another reason Jesus called the man to silence was to reduce the sensational impact of such miracles. It proved to be futile. As Mark writes, "He went out and began to talk freely about it, and to spread the news, so that Jesus could no longer openly enter a town, but was out in desolate places, and people were coming to him from every quarter" (Mark 1:45).

"Just Say the Word": Grace Includes the Unacceptable

When he had entered Capernaum, a centurion came forward to him, appealing to him, "Lord, my servant is lying paralyzed at home, suffering terribly." And he said to him, "I will come and heal him." But the centurion replied, "Lord, I am not worthy to have you come under my roof, but only say the word, and my servant will be healed. For I too am a man under authority, with soldiers under me. And I say to one, 'Go,' and he goes, and to another, 'Come,' and he comes, and to my servant, 'Do this,' and he does it." When Jesus heard this, he marveled and said to those who followed him, "Truly, I tell you, with no one in Israel have I found such faith. I tell you, many will come from east and west and recline at table with Abraham, Isaac, and Jacob in the kingdom of heaven, while the sons of the kingdom will be thrown into the outer darkness. In that place there will be weeping and gnashing of teeth." And to the centurion Jesus said, "Go; let it be done for you as you have believed." And the servant was healed at that very moment. (Matthew 8:5–13)

Throughout His Galilean ministry, the Lord used Capernaum as His base of operations. It was a border town, within the territory of Herod Antipas but close to the jurisdiction of his half brother Herod Philip, both sons of Herod the Great. It was also a crossroads town, situated by important international trade routes. As a result, although it was primarily Jewish, it had a diverse population for political and business reasons, including tax collection. Its strategic location also made it an obvious place for a Roman garrison. So it is not a surprise to find a centurion crossing paths with Jesus in Capernaum.

Centurions were, in many ways, the backbone of the Roman military. A centurion was the highest ranking noncommissioned Roman officer, technically the officer over one hundred men, though a typical *centuria* had about eighty men. In a relatively small garrison, such as that in Capernaum, he would probably be the ranking officer. He was the local embodiment of Roman power and, as such, would be both feared and resented as the symbol of Israel's status as an occupied country. It is somewhat surprising, therefore, to discover that the seven different centurions mentioned in the New Testament are all viewed in a positive light, with one of them—Cornelius—becoming the first Gentile to experience the fullness of Christ's salvation (Acts 10).

The centurion in Matthew's account is not named, but his unique relationship to the local community is mentioned. Despite his power and position, he was every bit the outsider that the leper was, a Gentile with no claim on the covenant promises of God. Yet this particular man was regarded with gratitude, respect, and even affection by the local leaders. In fact, Luke's more detailed account of the story tells us that the local Jewish leadership initiated his approach to Jesus, urging Jesus to pay attention to his request: "They pleaded with him earnestly, saying, 'He is worthy to have you do this for him, for he loves our nation, and he is the one who built us our synagogue'" (Luke 7:4–5).[5]

It is hardly surprising that the officer knew of Jesus. After all, it was his business to keep his finger on the pulse of the community, and news of Jesus was everywhere. It was highly unusual, however, for a representative of Rome to humbly petition for help from a popular Jewish teacher, especially one who was viewed with great alarm by the Jewish authorities. But he was completely uninterested in saving face or following conventional social protocol. A servant he greatly valued was "lying paralyzed at home, suffering terribly" (Matthew 8:6). Luke tells us that he was "sick and at the point of death" (Luke 7:2). It reveals something important about the soldier's character that he was distressed about the impending death of one of his servants. Intriguingly, he didn't even make a request of Jesus; he simply announced the urgency of the situation, making his distress clear: "Lord, my servant is lying paralyzed at home, suffering terribly" (Matthew 8:6). His faith and his restraint are remarkable. He was convinced that Jesus was fully capable of resolving the desperate situation. At the same time, he asserted no privileges and offered no enticements. He humbly laid the matter before the Lord. He was convinced that informing the Lord was enough. He did not need to bribe, convince, or coerce Him. There are lessons in prayer to be learned from this man!

Jesus's response was immediate: "I will come and heal him" (v. 7). In itself, this was a gracious response. In Jewish eyes, Jesus would make himself unclean merely by entering a Gentile home, since it would be "contaminated" by its lack of adherence to Jewish practices of ritual cleanliness. But once again the story takes an unexpected turn—the centurion tried to talk Jesus out of coming! His concern wasn't ritual contamination, but a remarkable recognition of the moral and spiritual superiority of the Lord Jesus. "I am not worthy to have you come under my roof," he declared (v. 8). A Roman officer saying to a Jewish peasant that he isn't "worthy"? Rome ruled the world and loved to assert its dominance. Subject peoples, including Jews, needed to know and keep their place. The whole system of Roman oppression was designed to make their superiority clear. Even the local leaders deferred to this man. Luke tells us that they had praised him to Jesus with the affirmation, "He is worthy to have you do this for him" (Luke 7:4). But this soldier operated on a very different scale. He knew that, next to Jesus, he was the unworthy one. Remember, this was a public discussion. Before witnesses, this powerful Roman had publicly humbled himself. This is genuine humility, and the divine principle remains true: "God opposes the proud but gives grace to the humble" (1 Peter 5:5; James 4:6; compare Proverbs 3:34).

The centurion followed his declaration of unworthiness with a remarkable comparison: "Only say the word, and my servant will be healed. For I too am a man under authority, with soldiers under me. And I say to one, 'Go,' and he goes, and to another, 'Come,' and he comes, and to my servant, 'Do this,' and he does it" (Matthew 8:8–9). This man actually believed that Jesus could speak a word of healing in one place and it would have power in another! Drawing upon his own experience as a military officer, he knew the power of commands issued by superior officers. When he spoke, he knew his men would obey. But it is one thing to have power over soldiers; it is quite another to have power over sickness and impending death. His statement is a confession of faith that Jesus has supreme power, the kind of power possessed by God himself. If the Lord had that kind of power, He could heal his servant, and He could do so without taking a single step closer to him!

The centurion certainly didn't have a comprehensive understanding of Jesus's true identity at this point in time. In truth, not even His closest disciples did. Yet he knew that Jesus belonged in a category entirely His own. Still, even he was not prepared for what was about to happen.

The Lord's first response was to praise this man's faith in the presence of this Jewish crowd. Only twice in the Gospels is the Lord said to show amazement. In Mark 6, Mark describes the Lord teaching in the synagogue in His hometown of Nazareth, only to be received with skepticism and rejection. Mark concludes with the observation, "And he marveled because of their unbelief" (Mark 6:6). Now Matthew tells us that Jesus, as He stood in His adopted hometown of Capernaum, "marveled" at the man's faith, his confidence that the Lord could deal with a life-threatening condition and heal his servant by simply speaking a word at a distance: "Truly, I tell you, with no one in Israel have I found such faith" (Matthew 8:10). The uniqueness of his faith goes beyond his belief that Jesus could heal whatever affliction at a distance. The man had come to realize that Jesus stood in an utterly unique relationship to God himself. Israel disbelieves, while a Gentile believes. What a strange reversal of expected responses to God's Messiah.

The Lord seized on that fact to challenge one of the most cherished beliefs of His contemporaries, that the mere fact of Jewish identity—or the meticulous practice of Jewish traditions—would be the basis for entry into God's kingdom. When Messiah comes, the rabbis taught, God's covenant people would have the privilege of entering into the promised kingdom of God, sharing the moment with Israel's patriarchs, Abraham, Isaac, and Jacob. The Lord's words challenge that anticipation head-on. It is faith that marks the true people of God, not just ethnic identity. As His eyes swept over the pressing crowds, He made an ominous declaration that must have stunned His hearers: "I tell you, many will come from east and west and recline at table with Abraham, Isaac, and Jacob in the kingdom of heaven, while the sons of the kingdom will be thrown into the outer darkness. In that place there will be weeping and gnashing of teeth" (vv. 11–12).

For the rabbis, the kingdom was a blessing for Jewish people; for Jesus it is a blessing for believers in Him. Jewish identity may be significant, but it was not enough, and by their unbelief, many Jews would experience the judgment of exclusion from God's kingdom. This would have been profoundly inconceivable, and even insulting, for most of those listening to Jesus. Jews thought of themselves as de facto heirs of the divine promises. Jesus makes it clear that only those who put their trust in Him will receive those promises; many Gentiles not only will enter the kingdom but will enjoy high privilege within it.

How the crowds responded to that declaration we can only imagine. Almost certainly a ripple of surprise, even mounting anger, swept through the gathered throng. But Jesus had turned His attention elsewhere. Fixing His eyes on the centurion, He simply declared, "Go; let it be done for you as you have believed" (v. 13). As we have seen before, there is no prayer or ritual, just a simple declaration that the man's request for the healing of his servant has been granted.

I love the simplicity of the story's ending: "And the servant was healed at that moment." Of course he was. But the servant's healing was not caused by the centurion's faith. It was caused by the Lord's power—His choosing to respond in grace to a man who believed in Him but could only declare his unworthiness to receive what he was asking for. This is, of course, the very essence of saving faith.

These two miracles involve people who were different in almost every way. The first was a Jewish outcast, suffering from an incurable, socially marginalizing illness and shunned by all. The second was also an outsider but in a very different way—a Gentile outsider, at the top of the local power structure, with the earned respect of his community. Yet with all his prominence, he was still an outsider, and no observant Jew would dare to enter his house. But there are no "untouchables" with Jesus. It doesn't matter how others see us; what matters is how we see the Lord and how the Lord sees us. He is a Savior whose grace touches the untouchable and embraces the unacceptable.

But, if there are no incurables, there are also no specially privileged. It was, and is, a great privilege to be able to trace your ancestry back to Abraham, Isaac, and Jacob. Or, in our case, to boast a family legacy of people of faith, who knew, trusted, and followed the Lord Jesus. In a certain sense, we can see ourselves as "sons of the kingdom" (v. 12), with guaranteed kingdom rights, as these people did. But spiritual genealogy does not secure heaven; only faith in the Lord Jesus does. A terrible eternity awaits those who trust in anything other than the person and work of Christ. But a glorious eternity in the kingdom of the Lord Christ awaits those who trust in Him. Are you among them?

The two miracles demonstrate something about the nature of faith. While both men did not have perfectly formed understandings of Jesus, they both came with faith and trust that He was able to meet their needs, even though they could do nothing to deserve His help. They came empty-handed, with the confidence that He would hear and respond. And they took Him at His word. This is the kind of faith that receives the far greater gifts of eternal life and salvation.

We are also reminded, in both cases, that the Lord's power is wedded to His compassion. For Christ-followers, the way we see people must be the way the Lord Jesus saw and treated people. It must move us toward the hurting and the broken, not away from them. We live in a society saturated with consumerism, one that teaches us to ask, "What can you do for me?" The more closely we follow Christ, the more we will reverse the question, seeking to show His compassion to those in need around us.

FIVE

FIRST THINGS FIRST

On December 29, 1972, Eastern Airlines Flight 401 took off from Kennedy Airport, headed for Miami, Florida. The flight was routine, but toward the end of the flight, when the pilots deployed the landing gear, a tiny green light failed to flash back at them. This light should have affirmed that the gear was locked in place, so they put the plane on autopilot and focused on their problem. Unfortunately, they became so engrossed in the project that they failed to hear a warning tone indicating that the plane had deviated from their selected altitude. It was dark outside, so there were no visible indicators outside the cockpit windows alerting them to their peril as the plane continued to descend. Within minutes, the plane crashed into the Florida Everglades, taking the lives of 101 of the 176 passengers and crew.

An old maxim reminds us, "The main thing is to keep the main thing the main thing." A pilot's chief task is to fly the plane, an obvious fact these pilots tragically forgot. It is a principle that applies to each one of us and to all of life. Immediate demands may not be essential, and pressing needs aren't always primary. We too easily confuse the urgent with the important, to our own peril and the peril of others.

The Lord Jesus never confused the two. He was able to meet people's present felt needs but also their deepest needs. He came to deal not merely with the symptoms of our problems but with the source of them, a truth clearly on display in the miracle account before us in this chapter. A man was brought to Jesus with an obvious and pressing need that had made his entire life a special burden. As the Lord Jesus dealt with that need, He made it clear that He had the power to deal with the man's deepest need. In so doing, He made an audacious claim that revealed His true identity.

> And when he returned to Capernaum after some days, it was reported that he was at home. And many were gathered together, so that there was no more room, not even at the door. And he was preaching the word to them. And they came, bringing to him a paralytic carried by four men. And when they could not get near him because of the crowd, they removed the roof above him, and when they had made an opening, they let down the bed on which the paralytic lay. And when Jesus saw their faith, he said to the paralytic, "Son, your sins are forgiven." Now some of the scribes were sitting there, questioning in their hearts, "Why does this man speak like that? He is blaspheming! Who can forgive sins but God alone?" And immediately Jesus, perceiving in his spirit that they thus questioned within themselves, said to them, "Why do you question these things in your hearts? Which is easier, to say to the paralytic, 'Your sins are forgiven,' or to say, 'Rise, take up your bed and walk'? But that you may know that the Son of Man has authority on earth to

forgive sins"—he said to the paralytic—"I say to you, rise, pick up your bed, and go home." And he rose and immediately picked up his bed and went out before them all, so that they were all amazed and glorified God, saying, "We never saw anything like this!" (Mark 2:1–12)

My wife has a great love for the birds that grace our back yard when spring comes. And she delights to provide seed to entice more to join them. The only problem is that our area abounds in squirrels, beautiful enough in themselves but also cunning and skillful when it comes to emptying our birdfeeder. My wife spends a great deal of energy trying to outwit them, but her victories usually prove to be short-lived. The squirrels are relentless. The same feed that attracts the birds also draws the rodents.

This miracle in Mark 2 illustrates the same dynamic in the ministry of Jesus. It is one of the best-known and most beloved of Jesus's miracles, told in each of the first three gospels. Many will remember Sunday school teachers creatively relating the story of four men digging through the roof of a house to get their paralyzed friend to Jesus, who then miraculously heals him. It is a compelling scene for its drama. But more importantly, it marks a major turning point in the ministry of Jesus.

He is once again in a home in Capernaum, His adopted hometown, the scene of many of His miracles. But with this miracle, things begin to take a darker turn. Mark places this as the first of a series of five episodes in which Jesus comes in direct and deepening conflict with the Jewish religious authorities. Jesus's miracles were wonderful for those who were on the receiving end. But for others, the visibility and credibility they gave to Jesus was deeply threatening. They didn't see Jesus as kind and compassionate, but as ominous and dangerous.

Declaring Forgiveness: "Your Sins Are Forgiven"

As we approach the story, there are some things we don't know. For example, we don't know how much time has elapsed since the miracles recorded earlier took place. It is, however, obvious that the buzz created by Jesus's remarkable miracles and teaching is only increasing. So, when word gets out that He is back in town in a certain house, hurting, hopeful, and curious people began to converge on it.

We are also not told whose house it was—Peter's? The one Jesus lived in? The house of a willing host? We can't be sure and don't need to know. We can, however, be fairly sure it was a typical Galilean house: relatively small with only a few rooms, one story high, made primarily of basalt, with an outside staircase leading to a flat roof. It wouldn't take many people to crowd out such a house, and before long, people were spilling out the door and onto the street, straining to hear whatever Jesus was saying and stretching to see whatever He might be doing.

Suddenly there arrived on the scene a paralyzed man, lying on a mat carried by four of his friends. Perhaps they had missed Jesus's earlier healing sessions, but they had certainly learned of them and were determined not to miss this opportunity. We are not told the nature of the man's condition. Was it a birth defect? The result of a terrible accident? The aftermath of some illness? Whatever the cause, two things are obvious. First, his condition was irreversible and incurable. Nothing available to practitioners of first-century medicine could offer the slightest possibility of hope. Second, he was a man entirely dependent on others in nearly every area of his life, yet he was blessed with some very faithful and determined friends. On his own, he had no way of getting to Jesus. They made it possible.

His friends had no intention of letting the overflowing and tightly packed crowds prevent them from getting the paralyzed man to Jesus. Their belief that Jesus could make a difference is evident from what they chose to do. Seeing the crowds and the impossibility of pushing their way through, they adopted a highly creative and very daring plan, a plan that could very well have earned them intense disapproval and economic liability. Skirting the crowds, they climbed the stairs to the flat roof, carrying their friend. The roof itself was made of beams, overlaid with straw and branches, and covered with mud.[1] Luke tells us that there were also tiles (Luke 5:19). So they laid their friend down and calculated where they would need to begin making a hole, through which they could lower their friend on his stretcher down to Jesus. We can only imagine the consternation and probably anger beneath them as dirt, straw, and other debris began to tumble on the crowds below.

Then came the moment their purpose became clear, as they carefully began to lower their paralyzed friend to the feet of Jesus. It is a marvelous picture, and we can only imagine the impression it made on everyone standing down below, especially on the man who owned the house!

We should pause here for a few moments. When the friends stood on that rooftop pondering their next step, they were faced with a major question. Up to this point, people would have been impressed by their commitment to their friend and sympathetic to their cause. But now they were about to demolish a major part of someone's home. We know how we would react were someone to attempt forceful entry into our home by destroying part of it. There is no reason to suspect the owner of this house would have felt differently. To dig open someone else's roof would expose them to both financial liability and significant social stigma—not to mention the weather. But their strong concern for their friend and their deep confidence in Jesus's ability to transform his future overrode their hesitation and drove them to radical action.

Obviously the man's friends are only secondary to the story. Placing our emphasis on them and not on Jesus would be a great mistake. But in their actions there is a challenge for those of us who are Christ-followers. They knew that their friend had no hope of healing other than through Jesus. They also knew that their friend had no way to get to Jesus on his own. Their love for him made them willing to make the effort and take the risk, if only to get him to the only one who could meet his need. We must never forget that all of our friends and acquaintances who do not yet know Jesus have a need far greater than paralysis. Only Jesus can save them from their spiritual condition before a holy God. The example of these friends should convict and inspire us to do whatever is necessary to get everyone we know to the Lord Jesus.

The Lord's response to the man now in front of Him was both immediate and surprising: "Son, your sins are forgiven" (Mark 2:5). We should first notice that the Lord said this because He had seen and recognized their faith, almost certainly the faith of both the paralyzed man and his friends. Their faith had an object—Jesus. How much they knew about Him is unclear, but they clearly believed He had supernatural power beyond human capacity, a power that could transform their paralyzed friend's life. Their faith is evident not only in what they believed about Jesus but also in what they did on the basis of that belief. At great effort and potential risk, they had done what they could to get their friend and his need to Jesus. True faith isn't merely assent to truth about Jesus; it is active trust in Him.

Still, they hadn't come to Jesus so that their friend could be forgiven. They wanted him to be able to walk. Their evaluation of his need was purely physical. So I suspect they were startled and even disappointed when Jesus pronounced him forgiven. They had come with a very clear idea of what they wanted Jesus to do for him, and had worked hard to get him there. But Jesus seemingly ignored the man's obvious and very significant problem, and addressed something else entirely. He declared him forgiven, not healed. Some suggest that Jesus talked about forgiving sins because the man's paralysis was a divine judgment for some sin. While that is possible, there is no evidence of it in this story. It is far more likely that Jesus was looking beyond the man's present and very real need to penetrate to his (and everyone's) primary need—forgiveness before a holy God. That, supremely, is why the Lord Jesus had come into the world. As the angel had told Joseph: "You shall call his name Jesus, for he will save his people from their sins" (Matthew 1:21).

Jesus spoke to that need clearly and crisply. It would be a great thing were the man to become paralysis-free, but it is a much greater thing to be guilt-free. His greatest need, like ours, was not the most obvious one. His deepest desire was to be able to walk: If only I could walk, then my life would be fine. I'd be satisfied. Just do that for me, and I'll be fine. We are just like that: Lord, if only I had this removal of an illness or a problem, this relationship, this restoration of my marriage, this job, this house . . .

But the Lord knew exactly what He was doing, to give him what he needed most. We should also recognize that the Lord's pronouncement was a personally costly one. Sins don't magically disappear, like pushing the delete button on a computer. A righteous God must deal with sins righteously, and that required Jesus's own death on the cross.

The Lord Jesus had another purpose for speaking as He did. When Jesus declared the man forgiven, He was claiming for himself a prerogative that belongs to God alone: the authority to forgive sins! He knew exactly the effect that proclamation would have on the suspicious ears of the theological watchdogs who surrounded Him, ready to pounce on any deviation from their theological paradigm. That is exactly what happened.

Declaring Forgiveness: "Who Can Forgive Sins but God Alone?"
Jesus's words and actions had not been going unnoticed by the
theological establishment. In fact, in Luke's account of this story,
he tells us, "Pharisees and teachers of the law were sitting there, who
had come from every village of Galilee and Judea and from Jerusalem" (Luke 5:17). If some of them had come all the way north from
Jerusalem to Galilee, they almost certainly represented an investigative committee, not an accidental gathering of theologians. The
teachers of the law were theological experts, in this case from the
party of the Pharisees, who were deeply concerned about theological orthodoxy. Jesus's words were intentionally scandalous and even
subversive to these religious authorities.

When Jesus announced, "Son, your sins are forgiven," all their
theological alarm bells went off. They realized the full implications
of what Jesus was asserting. Perhaps a priest could pronounce forgiveness when a person had offered a sacrifice at the temple, but
he would only be speaking as God's representative. This Teacher,
however, had the audacity to declare a man's sins forgiven on the
basis of His own authority. The claim was not just audacious; it was
blasphemous.

Mark tells us that individually they all thought the same thing:
"Why does this man speak like that? He is blaspheming! Who can
forgive sins but God alone?" (2:7). It didn't take long for those
inward thoughts to become increasingly loud murmurs of annoyance, disapproval, and complaint to one another. This Jesus
wasn't claiming to forgive a person for some sin committed against
Him, nor was He offering forgiveness for some particular act.
He was actually daring to declare a blanket forgiveness for all the
man's sins, surely something that only God could do. Their logic
was solidly biblical, resting on three assertions. First, only the one
sinned against can forgive the offender. I may be able to forgive
someone who sins against me, but I can hardly forgive a person who

has sinned against someone else. A third party has no legitimacy to confer forgiveness. Second, all sin is ultimately against God. Third, only God can forgive all sins, since only God knows all sins and all sins are ultimately against Him.[2]

Their reasoning was accurate, and their conclusion was ominous: Jesus was claiming to be able to do what only God can do. He was therefore guilty of the supreme sin: blasphemy. Such dishonoring of God was not a trivial offense, but a capital one, for which the law of Moses prescribed the penalty of stoning (Leviticus 24:16).

The mood in that house had suddenly taken a dark and ominous turn, as the festering anger of the Jewish leaders began to erupt. Jesus was fully aware of their increasingly virulent reaction. Mark tells us that He immediately perceived "in his spirit" their objection (Mark 2:8). While this may refer to His supernatural insight, it may also refer to an awareness of their intensifying murmurs and increasingly aggressive body language. But His response was not to back down from His declaration, to claim, in the mode of a modern politician, that He had misspoken or been misunderstood. Instead, He countered their question with a question of His own: "Which is easier, to say to the paralytic, 'Your sins are forgiven,' or to say, 'Rise, take up your bed and walk'?" (v. 9).

The question is a fascinating one. Obviously, neither healing nor forgiveness is easy in and of themselves. On the one hand, it is obviously easier to say "Your sins are forgiven" because there is no way, this side of heaven, to prove whether or not that declaration is valid. How can you prove or disprove such a claim? On the other hand, the efficacy of a command to "rise up and walk" is instantly verifiable. The paralytic either will or he won't. Yet, while declaring forgiveness may be "easier" than declaring someone healed, providing forgiveness for sins is an entirely different matter. Jesus could only declare the man's sins forgiven because He himself would provide the sacrifice on the cross that would make full and final forgiveness possible. It was something only He, as the God-man, could do.

But that aspect of Jesus's claim to authority remained hidden for the time being. He would now verify His claim of divine authority to forgive sins by revealing His authority over the effects of sin, this man's paralysis: "But that you may know that the Son of Man has authority on earth to forgive sins" (v. 10). This is the first time in Mark that the Lord has used His favorite title for himself, "Son of Man." On one level, it simply means "human being." But on a more profound level, the Lord Jesus was taking the title from Daniel 7:13–14. There, "one like a son of man" is a heavenly being who approaches the throne of God and is given kingly authority over the entire earth. Increasingly, Jesus will use this title in his ministry to describe himself as God's Messiah, the coming King. Still, it was a vague enough term that it didn't carry all the political and theological baggage that "Messiah" did for Jews living under Roman occupation.

The Lord Jesus was claiming not only the ability but also the authority to forgive sins on the earth. In other words, He was claiming for himself the prerogative of God. He will make that "incredible" claim credible by giving the grumbling religious leaders a visible display of His divine authority in the spiritual realm by demonstrating His authority in the physical realm. His healing power was not an end in itself. It was a flashing arrow, pointing to His divine authority. In what He was about to do, there was an implicit claim to deity.

The Lord suddenly turned His attention back to the paralyzed man, lying expectantly on his mat at Jesus's feet: "I say to you, rise, pick up your bed, and go home" (Mark 2:11). There was no turning back: either the man would remain as he was, or Jesus was demonstrating the authority He had claimed. The man had been commanded to do what was obviously impossible for him to do—to rise and walk. Even if he hadn't been paralyzed, the bedridden man's muscles would have atrophied over time to the point where there would have been no possibility of him standing, never mind walking. Jesus didn't pull the man up by his hand. Friends didn't rush to help him stand tall. I like the way Luke, with his physician's eye, describes what happened next: "And immediately he rose up before them and picked up what he had been lying on and went home, glorifying God" (Luke 5:25).

What a walk home that must have been, rejoicing with his friends as they danced through the streets to astonish the man's family! His immediate delight was almost certainly that he could walk and enter once again into regular life, free of restraint. He had been instantly and completely healed. And, perhaps in hindsight, he would come to realize that the spiritual healing through the Lord's forgiveness had been an even greater healing than what had happened to him physically. Perhaps, several years later, he came to realize that the Lord Jesus, who had declared the forgiveness of his sins, had died on the cross to provide for that very forgiveness through His atoning death.

The effect on the crowd was electric: "And amazement seized them all, and they glorified God and were filled with awe, saying, 'We have seen extraordinary things today'" (Luke 5:26). The man's renewed ability was undeniable, irrefutable, and unexplainable, except on the basis of the supernatural ability of the Lord Jesus. But in a profound way, most of the people were astonished at the wrong thing. The really amazing thing was not a paralyzed man walking, but the God-man living among them!

For another group, the effect of the miracle was very different. The Lord's miracle didn't answer their objections; it enflamed their animosity. The same Jewish leaders who had murmured at Jesus's words refused to see what was clearly before them. In fact, the encounter only hardened their desire to destroy Him. Only one chapter later in Mark's gospel, we will read that "the Pharisees went out and immediately held counsel with the Herodians against him, how to destroy him" (Mark 3:6). The statement is remarkable. The Pharisees and the Herodians were bitter political, religious, and cultural enemies, the Pharisees loyal to Jewish tradition, the Herodians to Herod and Gentile culture. The only thing the two groups agreed on was that Jesus was a dangerous threat to both of them; He had to be eliminated.

Looking back at the story, there are at least three things we should observe. *First, the miracle is a reminder of our deepest need.* In the eyes of the paralytic and his friends, the man's greatest need was to get to Jesus so that his paralysis could be healed. That was a noble desire. But the Lord Jesus abruptly reminded them—and us—that our primary need is for our sin to be forgiven by a holy God. Paralysis will not keep us out of heaven, but sin will. Jesus came to do for us not just what we want most, but what we need most and cannot do for ourselves. The question arises, if you were in this man's position, which would you rather hear: "Pick up your bed and go home" or "Your sins are forgiven"? In the midst of our present pain, most of us would choose the former. In the reality of our eternal destiny, all of us need the forgiveness that only the Lord Jesus can provide.

Second, the miracle gives insight into Jesus's true identity. The miracle points to His supreme power; the forgiveness points to His divine nature. The Lord Jesus performed this miracle to validate His claim that He possesses the right to do what only God has the right to do—forgive sins. In Matthew 11:27, Jesus claims that the Father has handed over all things to Him. In John 5, He claims the ability to do all that He sees God doing, including raising the dead (v. 21). And He says that the Father has given Him the right to judge all people (v. 22). He also claims for himself God's unique name, "I am" (John 8:58; see Exodus 3:14), and asserts that He possessed glory with His Father before all creation (John 17:5). These astonishing revelations of His identity are beginning to be unveiled in this miracle.

Third, the miracle suggests the immense cost of our salvation. The Lord healed this man by a word of sovereign power. He spoke, and the paralysis was gone. He also forgave the man by a declaration of forgiveness, but for that forgiveness to be fully operative, He gave His life on the cross. He did not simply decree forgiveness; He bore the penalty of our sin by paying the price. Only the offended party can forgive the offender, and He does so at a cost to himself. Were you to forgive me of a financial debt, you would, in fact, be taking the economic cost upon yourself. The One I have sinned against has taken the cost of that sin upon himself, so that "the blood of Jesus his Son cleanses us from all sin" (1 John 1:7).

Fourth, we witness in the miracle the blindness of unbelief. The Jewish leaders heard the logic; they saw the miracle; they saw the wonder of the surrounding crowds who "glorified God saying, 'We never saw anything like this!'" (Mark 2:12). But they didn't glorify God, although they couldn't deny what they had seen. Instead, they doubled down on their refusal to see Jesus for who He truly is. It is a vivid reminder that only God can open blind eyes, and that the miracle of salvation is even more amazing than the healing of a paralyzed man. It is also a sad pattern we will see repeated again and again in the responses of the Jewish leaders to Jesus's miracles. There are none so spiritually blind as those who will not see.

SIX

STORM LESSONS

It doesn't matter where you live. Sooner or later, you are going to find yourself in a storm. They come in all forms—windstorms, hailstorms, dust storms, snowstorms, rainstorms, firestorms, hurricanes, tornadoes, and the list goes on. Even as I write this, the television news reports are filled with accounts of a devastating storm creating enormous havoc on an almost unbelievable scale. Fortunately, meteorologists are often able to predict the approach of a dangerous storm with considerable accuracy, enabling us to make appropriate preparations. But some storms come unexpectedly, either in location or ferocity, often leaving in their wake a trail of death, destruction, and heartbreak.

Storms are an inevitable part of life. Wise people, therefore, prepare for and protect against them, to the best of their ability. Being ready for the storm is simply practical wisdom. The Lord Jesus used this fact of life to illustrate the difference between a wise person and a fool in His famous parable: The wise man built his house on a rock, the fool on sand. The results were dramatically different when the storm hit (see Matthew 7:24–28).

Of course, the Lord Jesus wasn't giving construction advice, but life advice. He was reminding us of what we should know. Weather storms illustrate life storms: they are inevitable but often very unpredictable. Truth be told, we often give more diligence to preparing for nature's storms than for personal ones. They come in so many ways: a devastating medical diagnosis, a terrible accident, loss of employment, an economic downturn, the disintegration of a marriage, the destruction of a personal dream. . . . All at once, we find ourselves beyond our depth, with waves crashing over the sides of our boat, bailing furiously, trying to stay afloat, all the while fearing what will happen if our boat capsizes.

There are some folks who delight in being storm chasers. Whether for reasons of thrill-seeking or important scientific research, they put themselves in harm's way, often capturing cellphone videos that inspire awe and fear. I've never been tempted to join them—I'd rather be a storm avoider! But that isn't possible. Storms come, and some of them have stretched me to my very limits. In them, the Lord has proved to be both present and powerful, and the lessons I learned have been for my good and His glory.

There are certain things God can teach us in a storm that we cannot and will not learn any other way. And one of the Lord's best-known miracles occurs in this context. In the midst of the storm was a lesson not just for the benefit of His disciples who lived it, but for us who have been given the opportunity to observe them. Each of the first three gospels recounts the story; we will view it primarily through Mark's eyes.

On that day, when evening had come, he said to them, "Let us go across to the other side." And leaving the crowd, they took him with them in the boat, just as he was. And other boats were with him. (Mark 4:35–36)

The miracles of the Lord Jesus that we have observed so far have not only met human needs; they have aroused faith in His disciples and opposition in His adversaries. The four miracles that we will consider in the next three chapters occur together in Mark's gospel, as the Lord continues to move around the shores of Lake Galilee. They graphically display the power and person of the Lord Jesus, as He rules over the forces of nature, the powers of evil, and the presence of disease and even death.

A Calm Sea under a Clear Sky

One of the dangers of looking at a story like this is that we tend to read it in isolation from the context in which the gospel writer narrates it. As a result, we miss the larger significance of the story. So, as we unpack this event, we need to notice that it comes at the end of a busy day of ministry for Jesus and His disciples. In the earlier part of chapter 4, Mark had described what we might call "a day of parables," as Jesus addressed large crowds by the shore of Lake Galilee. Mark has made it clear in his third chapter that the Lord Jesus is encountering growing opposition from the Jewish leaders, opposition that we have seen was intensified by His dramatic healing of the paralyzed man in the middle of a debate about Jesus's claim to be able to forgive sins. It had been a long day, and by late afternoon, Jesus and His disciples were exhausted from their ministry to the crowds. Ministry is often draining: people can be difficult and demanding, and that was true even for the Lord Jesus.

The Lord Jesus felt a need for He and the Twelve to go off on their own, to get away from the crowds for a time of retreat and refreshment. It is important to observe that *crossing the lake was Jesus's idea, not the disciples' idea.* He is the one who said: "Let us go across to the other side" (Mark 4:35). His suggestion wasn't impulsive, but intentional.

The suggestion immediately appealed to the disciples, and they didn't require any further encouragement. Jesus had been with them, sitting in a boat while He taught the crowds who lined the shore. So we are told, "They took him with them in the boat, just as he was" (v. 36). No special preparations; suddenly, off they went, just as they were.

Several details help us set the scene more accurately in our minds. We can have a good idea of the sort of boat they used because of a remarkable discovery in Lake Galilee in 1986. A drought had caused the water level of the lake to drop so much that it exposed a boat buried in the muddy lake bottom. Scientists dated the remains to the first century, leading to the nickname "the Jesus Boat," since it was from the very time and location frequented by Jesus and His disciples. Made of wood, twenty-eight feet long and eight feet wide, it would have been able to hold around fifteen people, perfectly sized for Jesus and the twelve disciples.

By now it was late afternoon or early evening, not the usual time for a crossing. But they set out anyway, as a group of other boats tagged along. Lake Galilee isn't a very large lake—about thirteen miles long and eight miles across at its widest, and at least four of Jesus's disciples were professional fishermen who knew the lake well. We can be sure that there was no evidence of an approaching storm that would have made the voyage unwise.

Jesus was exhausted after a long day of ministry, and His disciples were more than qualified to navigate their journey to the other side of the lake. So He curled up under the deck at the stern of the boat, having found some kind of cushion to use as a pillow, and quickly fell into a deep sleep. It is an important reminder of the true humanity of the Lord. He wasn't pretending to be tired or sleepy—He really was exhausted. Such human weakness stands in remarkable contrast to the awe-inspiring display of power that was soon to follow!

For the disciples, this must have seemed like a special moment. They were under a clear sky on a calm sea, enjoying one another and anticipating what the company of their remarkable leader would bring them next. It might have seemed like the perfect ending to a special day of seeing Jesus in action. Perhaps they talked with one another about the meaning of some of the parables He had told them earlier, or maybe they reflected on the reactions of the people to what they had heard.

A Sudden Storm and a Sovereign Lord

And a great windstorm arose, and the waves were breaking into the boat, so that the boat was already filling. But he was in the stern, asleep on the cushion. And they woke him and said to him, "Teacher, do you not care that we are per-ishing?" And he awoke and rebuked the wind and said to the sea, "Peace! Be still!" And the wind ceased, and there was a great calm. He said to them, "Why are you so afraid? Have you still no faith?" And they were filled with great fear and said to one another, "Who then is this, that even the wind and the sea obey him?"

They came to the other side of the sea, to the country of the Gerasenes. (Mark 4:37–5:1)

The calm was not to last. Lake Galilee is located in a geograph-ical bowl, more than 600 feet below sea level. The hills to the west lead to the coast of the Mediterranean Sea, while to the north, Mount Hermon rises more than 9,000 feet. To the immediate northeast lie the Golan Heights, a volcanic plateau about forty miles long and sixteen miles wide. At its highest, the plateau is about 2,900 feet above sea level, with slopes leading down to Lake Galilee. Rainstorms sweep in off the Mediterranean, but their approach is signaled by the appearance of darkening rain clouds. "If the storms were rainstorms, the disciples—many of whom were seasoned fishermen—would have recognized the developing rainclouds and impending threat and sought shelter in one of the harbors around the lake."[1] However, strong, even violent, windstorms often come sweeping off the Golan Heights "suddenly, without warning and with fierce winds. This explains why the veteran fishermen were so terrified."[2]

The gospel writers confirm this description. Mark and Luke use a Greek word for "windstorm" that often refers to gale force winds, even hurricanes, while Matthew uses the word *seismos*, which more commonly describes an earthquake. Almost instantly, the lake which had been the place several of the disciples made their living was now threatening to take their lives. A boat filled with thirteen grown men would sit very low in the water, and it would not have taken very long for waves to begin pouring into the boat so that it was in danger of being swamped. They probably tried their best to bail the water, but that would quickly prove to be futile. The very violence of the storm could have torn the wooden boat apart, and they were too far from shore to hope to reach land safely. I wonder how many of them could even swim.

Suddenly a pleasant afternoon on the lake had turned into a laboratory to teach some of life's important truths. The first is simple but significant: *Storms are an inevitable part of life.* Troubles come certainly and often unexpectedly. From the opening words of the Sermon on the Mount, the Lord had taught that lesson: "Blessed are you when others revile you and persecute you and utter all kinds of evil against you falsely on my account" (Matthew 5:11). One of the last statements He made to them before He went to the cross is similar: "In the world you will have tribulation" (John 16:33).

The same is true for all of us. Storms come in a variety of forms, but suddenly we can find that our lives are filled with whitecaps.

- The boss calls you in and tells you that a reorganization or merger means you no longer have a job.
- The doctor's office calls, telling you that a test has revealed something concerning. A follow-up appointment is urgent.
- You're using the computer when something unexpected shows up, revealing that your spouse or one of your children has been viewing something they shouldn't.
- A habit or practice you've so carefully hidden is suddenly exposed, and you can't hide or pretend any longer.
- A pandemic hits with astonishing speed, impacting almost every segment of our lives, bringing death and disease, as well as economic and relational turmoil.

Storms come whether we're Christians or not. And perhaps before you finish reading this book, you will find yourself facing a storm you didn't see coming and had no way to prepare for.

Closely connected to the first "storm truth" is a second: *Storms come even when we're obeying Jesus.* The disciples were on that lake and in that storm because they were following Jesus. It is obvious that many of the storms we find ourselves in come because of disobedience. There is no more obvious illustration than that of the Old Testament prophet Jonah. He tried to flee west when the Lord had commanded him to go east, and it took a deadly storm and a hungry fish to get him turned around. Even then, he wasn't content, and it took a scorching wind and a hungry worm to get him to finally listen.

But if the Jonah story is a reminder that some storms enter our lives as the consequences of our stubborn disobedience, the story of Job is a reminder that our sovereign God will sometimes allow us to experience storms although, and even because, we are obeying

Him. The Lord Jesus had an agenda for His disciples in that storm, to teach them something they were not going to learn in any other way. Lessons learned on that lake would stay with them for the rest of their lives, as they served Him in places and in ways they never could have imagined.

This same principle applies to us. We want it all cut and dried. We think, This storm must be due to sin or unbelief in my life. I must be doing something wrong, or the Lord wouldn't let this happen! How often I've heard people apply their simplistic and often insensitive, arrogant and unspiritual diagnosis to the trials another believer is enduring. It is always a good thing to search our hearts and to honestly examine ourselves before the Lord. But these disciples were in the storm because they were doing exactly what Jesus had asked them to do. It is often in the storm of trials that the Lord shapes our character, deepens our trust, and sharpens our vision. So, in the storm, we hear the words of Scripture: "Count it all joy, my brothers, when you meet trials of various kinds, for you know that the testing of your faith produces steadfastness. And let steadfastness have its full effect, that you may be perfect and complete, lacking in nothing" (James 1:2–4).

In the middle of that lake, with their boat filling with water, the disciples encountered another important truth: *Storms come to teach us that we're not in control.* For some on that little boat, that was a humbling lesson. The Twelve included landlubbers, but at least four of them were experienced fishermen. They each knew Lake Galilee like the back of their hand. Of all places, the lake was where they were most confident and most in control. But now, confronted by a storm that was beyond their experience, as well as beyond their control, they were filled with a sense of panic. Perhaps that is where the realities of life hit us hardest: when the storm hits an area of our strength or our expertise, and we realize that we're beyond our depths! It must have been a humbling thing for

Peter, the proud fisherman, to appeal for help to Jesus, who wasn't a fisherman but a carpenter. But the storm had driven him to admit that he wasn't in control.

Western society teaches us to be self-reliant and to take control of our own lives. We protect against risks in almost every way, doing everything we can to prepare for the storms. We guard our children and our finances; we plan out our futures. We take wise precautions. But then something happens—something we can't stop or change. A category-five hurricane has breached our levies. We need what only Jesus can do for us. It is a hard lesson to learn, but also a wonderfully liberating one.

Remarkably, the disciples' instinctive reaction was to blame Jesus. Shaking Him out of His slumber, they challenged Him directly: "Teacher, do you not care that we are perishing?" (Mark 4:38). Their words hold some unstated assumptions. One is that if Jesus knew what was happening, He wouldn't have let them go through something like this! If He really cared about them, He would be active, not asleep. What kind of leader stays asleep at a time like that? They wanted Him to do something, even if they weren't sure what it was. But His apparent indifference to their situation suddenly cast doubt on what they thought they knew about Him.

We are not unlike them; we are tempted to respond in exactly the same way. "Lord, why are you allowing this to happen? Don't you know? Don't you care? Don't you hear?" V. Raymond Edman is usually credited with words that have become etched on my mind since I first heard them: "Never doubt in the dark what God has showed you in the light." What applies in the dark also applies in the storm. Even when He seems to be sleeping, the Lord knows all that we are doing. As Charles Spurgeon declared, "I would sooner walk in the dark and hold hard to a promise of my God, than trust in the light of the brightest day that ever dawned."[3]

Jesus's response to the fears of His disciples shows the wisdom of those words.

The Lord Jesus immediately showed why He can be trusted: in storms we learn the supremacy and sufficiency of the Lord Jesus. The account is remarkable by its matter-of-factness: "He awoke and rebuked the wind and said to the sea, 'Peace! Be still!'" (v. 39). He spoke to the untamable forces of nature as if they were an out-of-control family pet: "Be quiet! Be muzzled!" He didn't pray to His Father, recite some traditional chant, or invoke some "higher power." He spoke on His own authority. He merely rebuked and commanded. We've seen this before when He issued commands to demons, disabilities, and diseases.

When Jesus speaks, demons submit and depart. When Jesus speaks, nature obeys. That evening on Lake Galilee, the result was an instantaneous calm. The troubled sea became as smooth as glass. Mark describes it as a "great calm." If you've been around lakes or oceans, you know that isn't normal. When winds cease, the energy it has aroused in the water takes time to disperse. Waves become gradually smaller; they don't instantly vanish. But when Jesus speaks, they do. The power of the words of Jesus is the same power that spoke the universe into existence. How foolish that a well-known liberal scholar of a past age could write, "By an amazing coincidence the storm happened to lull the moment Jesus spoke."[4] Such coincidences seem strangely common around the Lord Jesus!

In the storm, the true glory of Jesus was revealed. This kind of power over nature is ascribed only to God in the Old Testament. Jesus does what only God can do, as Psalm 107:28–31 declares:

Then they cried to the LORD in their trouble,
and he delivered them from their distress.
He made the storm be still,
and the waves of the sea were hushed.

Then they were glad that the waters were quiet,
and he brought them to their desired haven.
Let them thank the LORD for his steadfast love,
for his wondrous works to the children of man!

It hasn't been in the calms of life that I've most deeply learned the truth about the supremacy and sufficiency of the Lord Jesus; it's been in the storms: sitting on a hospital bed, either my own or the bed of someone I deeply love; standing by the graveside of a beloved daughter, parent, relative, or family friend; stepping up to do something beyond my capacities or my experiences; stepping back when I find myself in conflict or facing an interpersonal challenge; or staring at a financial challenge that far exceeds my present resources.

Some of these storms are too personal and private to recount, but as I walked through them I experienced the gracious provision of God, unexpected wisdom and strength to meet the demands of the situation, the unforeseen solution to an intractable problem, and the deep, inward sense of His presence and peace.

All of that leads to another great gift found in the storm. *Storms forge our faith by increasing our awe of Christ.* Having stilled the storm, Jesus turned to challenge His disciples: "Why are you so afraid? Have you still no faith?" (v. 40). The word for "afraid" used in this verse is penetrating: it suggests that they are cowards: "Why are you cowardly?" The word "still" presses the knife even deeper: "Why is it taking you so long to really trust Me?" They had seen the Lord's power in action so many times and been overwhelmed by His wisdom and insight. Yet, like us, their default position was doubt. The fact is, the greatest danger facing the disciples wasn't the storm; it was their unbelief!

As with us. Why does it take so long for us to "get it"? How many times must we experience His sufficiency, His supremacy, and

His faithfulness before we can simply rest in Him? Jesus doesn't ask us to deny the storm; that would be nonsense. But He does ask us to remember His person and His promises. As George Müller said, "The only way to learn strong faith is to endure great trials. I have learned my faith by standing firm amid severe testings." As we learn to rely upon the Lord's presence and power in the storm, He begins to strip away our unhealthy self-confidence and replace it with a robust God-confidence.

There is yet another truth buried in this story that we can easily miss because of the chapter division. We read in Mark 5:1, "They came to the other side of the sea." That is, of course, exactly the place Jesus had pointed them toward at the start of their voyage: "Let us go across to the other side" (4:35). *Storms won't keep us from the Lord's intended destination.* They have reached their target, although not quite in the way they had expected. And they were now different men than they were when they set out from the opposite shore. It is striking that Jesus's words have aroused in them an even greater fear than the storm had. But it is a very different kind of fear: "What kind of person is this that even the winds and the lake obey him?" (4:41, my translation). Fear of the storm had been replaced by a fear of the Lord himself. This is not the fear induced by terror or cowardice. Rather, it is the awe of reverence. So the "great storm" and the "great calm" have led to "great fear." One of the great lessons of life is to get our fears in the right order. When awe of God is greater than fear of the storm, we are in a good place.

The full answer to the disciples' question "What kind of person is this?" will only occur to them gradually. The Lord Jesus continued to shatter all their categories. He is far greater than they could possibly have imagined, and just when they thought they understood who He really was, He once again transcended their understanding of Him. Their greatest problem had been, and will continue to be, a view of Jesus far below what is worthy of Him!

And that is our greatest problem as well. The gift of the storm is the recognition that Jesus is greater than they had ever imagined.

In *Prince Caspian*, C. S. Lewis depicts the Pevensie children, who have become lost in Narnia trying to find their way to Prince Caspian's camp. On the way, the lion Aslan, Lewis's Christ figure, appears to Lucy, the youngest of the children. Delighted to see him again, she declares, "Aslan, you're bigger."

"That is because you are older, little one," answered he.

"Not because you are?"

"I am not. But every year you grow, you will find me bigger."[5]

So too it will be for us, as we meet our Lord Jesus in the storms of our lives, and hear His voice through His Word. Our understanding of His supremacy and sufficiency will grow exponentially.

The journey across the lake was entirely different from what the disciples had expected it to be. But once they reached the place the Lord had intended them to reach, on the other side of the lake, they were different men, with a deeper and richer understanding of Jesus. And I suspect that none of them would have traded what they had learned in that terrifying storm for a pleasant ride on a calm sea under a clear night sky!

This story resonated in a deep way with the early Christians. The whole issue of living through the storm wasn't theoretical for Mark's first readers. They faced real, life-threatening and escalating persecution in Rome, as well as the kinds of storms that come from all the other issues of life. And that is the reality for many of our brothers and sisters in Christ around the world, as you read this. The intensity of the storms some of them are facing as Christ-followers is far beyond the experience of most of us.

But living through storms isn't theoretical for us either, although, by God's grace, we do not face the overt persecution many Christ-followers do. I'm not a prophet, but I can confidently predict that, before this year is over, every reader of this book is going to find herself or himself in a storm of one degree or another. And some who read are there even now. So the lessons from the miracle of the Lord's calming of the storm are directly relevant to us. The Lord of the storm is our Lord, and He doesn't test our faith to break it, but to build it. Our great comfort is that if the Lord is in our boat, the boat won't sink, the storm won't last forever, and we will find ourselves just where the Lord intended us to arrive all along![6]

SEVEN

POWER ENCOUNTER

I remember reading, years ago, the account of a boy who had a famous athlete as his personal hero. Pictures of this particular athlete decorated his walls, and accounts of his exploits thrilled the boy's soul. In the course of time, he had the chance to meet his hero. In fact, the athlete became a good friend of his father's, and he joined the family on a number of occasions. The boy was the envy of all his friends, and yet, he noted, "The closer I got to him, the smaller he became."

He wasn't insulting his hero, whose athletic skills were undeniable. But, up close, his flaws became more evident and his persona less mysterious. So it is, even with the most outstanding of people. As the old proverb declares, "No man is a hero to his valet."

The very reverse happened with those who were closest to the Lord Jesus. The disciples had already reorganized their lives to follow and accompany Him. They knew from the outset that He was unlike any person they had ever met. When they listened to His words, they heard an authority unlike any other teacher. When they witnessed His deeds of power, they saw in Him a remarkable glory that only served to deepen their faith in Him (John 2:11). Even so, when He commanded seismic winds to stop and a raging lake to calm, and those impersonal powers of nature instantly obeyed, they were overwhelmed. As highly as they had regarded Him before, they realized they had seriously underestimated Him: "What sort of man is this, that even winds and sea obey him?" (Matthew 8:27). He is Lord over even the powers of nature!

The disciples' journey of discovery was far from over. Safely on the other side of Lake Galilee, they were about to encounter a darker, more mysterious and menacing kind of power—supernatural forces of evil and darkness. They had witnessed the Lord's power over the demonic realms before, but now they were to encounter those sinister powers to a much higher degree, embodied in a man trapped in horrendous and fear-raising bondage. In doing so, they would come to realize that the darker the power, the brighter the glory of the Lord Jesus shines.

Encountering the Powers of Darkness

> They came to the other side of the sea, to the country of the Gerasenes. And when Jesus had stepped out of the boat, immediately there met him out of the tombs a man with an unclean spirit. He lived among the tombs. And no one could bind him anymore, not even with a chain, for he had often been bound with shackles and chains, but he wrenched the chains apart, and he broke the shackles in pieces. No one had the strength to subdue him. Night and day among the tombs and on the mountains he was always crying out and cutting himself with stones. (Mark 5:1–5)

The Lord Jesus had brought the disciples safely through the storm to the eastern shore of Lake Galilee. They now found themselves in a foreign place, because they had landed in Gentile territory. This was not by accident; the Lord who controls winds and waters had not been accidentally blown off course. They were in pagan country by divine appointment for further training by the Lord. They did not know it at the time, but most of them would later spend much of their lives taking the gospel to Gentile lands and people. Their training on this day would involve the rescue of a man held in the deepest kind of spiritual bondage.

The region where they landed was a Roman territory called the Decapolis (v. 20), "Ten Cities," so named because the region featured ten sizeable Greco-Roman cities. This is the first recorded visit by Jesus to Gentile territory during His ministry with His disciples; it was a place considered out of bounds for observant Jews. We cannot know whether any of His disciples had ever been there previously. What we do know is that the population was overwhelmingly non-Jewish, and their lifestyle typically pagan, a fact vividly revealed by the huge herd of pigs in this story. This was certainly not a feature of Jewish life! Archaeologists have unearthed evidence that the area was home to the worship of Greek gods, with the attendant presence of widespread idolatry and pagan morality.

They landed near a little village named Gergesa, or Kursi, in the region of the Gerasenes. It was very small, and virtually vanished not long after this time, causing later copyists of the New Testament manuscripts to struggle with the place name.[1] However, after the Six-Day War, when the Israelis occupied the area and were building a new road along the east side of the lake, they discovered the ruins of a little town called Kursi in 1970. Jesus and His followers weren't in the village itself, but in its general region.

If the location itself wasn't enough to unsettle them, the man who immediately confronted them was—virtually naked, filthy, and crazed looking. Luke tells us that "for a long time he had worn no clothes" (Luke 8:27). As Mark Strauss wryly observes, "The only thing worse than a violent, demon-possessed lunatic is a *naked*, violent, demon-possessed lunatic."[2] They had encountered demonized people before, as we saw in chapter 3, but this man[3] represented the most extreme example of demonization to be found in the Bible. Homeless, driven from normal human society, he gave every evidence of being unhinged from reality. He was unpredictable, uncontrollable, and potentially very dangerous.

Mark gives us further information that the disciples could only have learned later. The demoniac had made his home in the tombs, which were probably small caves or above-ground stone structures, a choice of location that made him completely unclean in Jewish eyes. He was also caught in terrible bondage: "Night and day. . . always crying out and cutting himself with stones" (Mark 5:5). Trapped in his body, with the torment of a victim and the strength of a wild animal, he was terrifyingly powerful while being pathetically enslaved and self-destructive. He had terrorized those around him, who had tried futilely to restrain him: "No one could bind him anymore, not even with a chain, for he had often been bound with shackles and chains, but he wrenched the chains apart, and he broke the shackles in pieces" (vv. 3–4). So he lived isolated and feared. Who could blame ordinary people from keeping their distance? The entire picture is one of darkness and suffering, of uncleanness and death.

It is a sad fact of modern life that, even in the richest country in the world, thousands of people find themselves homeless. More than a few of them battle with severe mental illnesses, the damage caused by chemical addictions or the legacy of acute psychological stress of various kinds. Some of them might even share this man's problem—"an unclean spirit" (v. 2). Our instinct is to pull back from compassionate engagement, guarding ourselves against the uncertain outcome of such an encounter. I suspect that the disciples would have been quite happy if Jesus had chosen to ignore the man and instructed them to get back in the boat and head north into safer Jewish territory.

In chapter 2, we considered Jesus's encounter with a demonized man in the synagogue in Capernaum. In that context, we observed that a biblical worldview does not allow us to dismiss the idea of demons as superstition. The Bible insists that Satan and the powers of darkness are real, evil, and active in our modern world, although we often fail to recognize them. As Paul reminds us, "Satan disguises himself as an angel of light" (2 Corinthians 11:14). Jesus's ministry involved profound and prolonged encounters with Satan and his minions, and the Gospels recount six specific miracles involving Jesus's power over the demonic. There are also a number of more general declarations where we read, without further description, that He "cast out many demons" (Mark 1:34).

There is an unseen spiritual world. One segment of our culture dismisses the powers of darkness as a relic of a superstitious past, like belief in elves, fairies, and dragons. We live, we are told, in a world of scientific discovery that has banished such beliefs, and the idea of real personal evil is nonsensical. However, another segment of our culture is fascinated by the paranormal, convinced that it is benign and ought to be embraced—a world of psychics, spirit guides, channels, and ascended masters. The biblical worldview is very different. The powers of darkness are real, and they are not benign.

We are not, however, to fear them, but to follow Christ. C. S. Lewis put the situation memorably: "There are two equal and opposite errors into which our race can fall about the devils. One is to disbelieve in their existence. The other is to believe, and to feel an excessive and unhealthy interest in them. They themselves are equally pleased by both errors and hail a materialist and a magician with the same delight."[4] A truly biblical balance is essential.

The presence of Satan and his forces is a fact. But, as this story makes clear, *the Lord Jesus confronted and controlled the powers of darkness.* As His disciple John tells us, "The reason the Son of God appeared was to destroy the works of the devil" (1 John 3:8). He constantly confronted personal, spiritual forces of evil, and above all, Satan, the prince of the demonic forces. At the same time, the Bible carefully distinguishes the demonic from the natural. It doesn't simplistically lump what can't be easily explained or what seems bizarre into a category of "the demonic." Note the careful distinctions found in Matthew 4:24: "So his fame spread throughout all Syria, and they brought him all the sick, those afflicted with various diseases and pains, those oppressed by demons, those having seizures, and paralytics, and he healed them."

Undoubtedly, the mission of Jesus inspired a special outbreak of demonic opposition. But even today, *Christ-followers are involved in spiritual warfare.* Not all that people ascribe to the powers of darkness is really demonic. There is a huge realm of superstition and obsession. Some "experiences" are the products of super-charged emotions or fevered imagination. But that does not remove the reality of the evil one. Yet, the powers of evil do not work the same way in every time and culture. In our culture, the subtly demonic seems to be far more effective than the blatantly demonic.

We should also recognize that believers can come under demonic influence, even oppression. That is why the Bible warns us about things like unresolved anger and pride. I do not believe that Christians indwelt by the Holy Spirit can be demon possessed (1 John 4:4). But the warnings of the New Testament make it clear that we can certainly be oppressed and virtually overwhelmed by the agents of the evil one. Still, we must not be demon obsessed. *In the Lord Jesus, we have the power and the resources to overcome the powers of darkness.*

The Powers of Darkness Must Yield to the Power of Christ

> And when he saw Jesus from afar, he ran and fell down before him. And crying out with a loud voice, he said, "What have you to do with me, Jesus, Son of the Most High God? I adjure you by God, do not torment me." For he was saying to him, "Come out of the man, you unclean spirit!" And Jesus asked him, "What is your name?" He replied, "My name is Legion, for we are many." And he begged him earnestly not to send them out of the country. Now a great herd of pigs was feeding there on the hillside, and they begged him, saying, "Send us to the pigs; let us enter them." So he gave them permission. And the unclean spirits came out and entered the pigs; and the herd, numbering about two thousand, rushed down the steep bank into the sea and drowned in the sea. (Mark 5:6–13)

One of the remarkable aspects of this story is that it is the demonized man who seeks out the encounter with Jesus: "And when he saw Jesus from afar, he ran and fell down before him" (v. 6). His actions seem almost schizophrenic. On the one hand, he rushed toward Jesus, rather than running away from him. On the other hand, his words attempted to dismiss Jesus entirely. It is striking that the demons controlling the man knew immediately, without being told, both the name and nature of Jesus. My guess is that something deep within this tormented man drove him to Jesus as his only source of hope, while the demonic beings residing within him revolted at Jesus's very presence, demanding to be left alone.

The fact is that Jesus is unavoidable. With a striking unanimity, when demons encounter Jesus in the Gospels, they recognize Him for who He is, and are forced into an encounter they know they cannot possibly win. Earlier in Mark, when the demonized man

in the synagogue at Capernaum met Jesus, the demon had protested, "What have you to do with us, Jesus of Nazareth? Have you
come to destroy us? I know who you are—the Holy One of God"
(1:24). Here the protest is almost identical: "What have you
to do with me, Jesus, Son of the Most High God? I adjure you
by God, do not torment me" (5:7). They confess the true identity
of Jesus as God the Son, at the same time bearing witness to the
inevitability of their judgment at His hands. The irony is profound.
On the lake, after the storm, the disciples had responded with rev-
erent awe: "Who then is this, that even the wind and the sea obey
him?" (4:41). Now, on the shore, the demons respond with fear:
"What have you to do with me, Jesus, Son of the Most High God?"
The disciples must have been astounded!

We don't understand very much about the world of the demonic, and we may be tempted to try to fill in the blanks with
speculations, but such guesswork is both useless and often very dangerous. The Lord has revealed in His Word what we need to know.
As these demons' encounter with Jesus continued, it became clear
that they feared two things. First, they did not want to leave their
present territory. As Mark 5:10 indicates, "And he begged him earnestly not to send them out of the country." (The word translated
"country" in this verse is probably better rendered "region" or "territory.") We can only guess why. Second, they feared being disem-
bodied, and knowing that Jesus would not send them into other
humans, they begged Him, "Send us to the pigs; let us enter them"
(v. 12). Apparently a group of pigs, the epitome of what was unclean,
was their best alternative.

The Lord Jesus was in complete mastery of the situation, as totally unfazed by the presence of the demons as He had been by the
tumultuous storm. The demons recognized His authority and their
own ultimate doom. Matthew tells us that they cried out to Jesus
in protest: "Have you come here to torment us before the time?"

(Matthew 8:29), obviously referring to the realization that their final destiny under divine judgment was certain. Luke tells us that they begged Him "not to command them to depart into the abyss" (8:31), apparently referring to a place of intermediate divine judgment, before their eternal destination in the Lake of Fire. They knew that their time was limited, their doom was sure, and that the Lord Jesus was their ultimate Judge.

Their immediate destiny was also under His control: "Come out of the man, you unclean spirit!" (Mark 5:8). He then demanded the demon's name. We know from extrabiblical materials that this was a standard practice of people who claimed the ability to cast out demons, but this is the only time the Lord Jesus does this. Almost certainly, since He doesn't again do this, He did so to reveal to the disciples the extent of the man's bondage and the strength of the demonic forces arrayed against Him. "My name is Legion," came the reply, "for we are many" (v. 9). A Roman legion was not a small squadron, but a division of up to 6,000 soldiers. Jesus was facing an army of Satan's soldiers—one against 6,000!

Once again, Jesus merely issued a command: "Come out of the man, you unclean spirit!" (v. 8). He used none of the methods of the so-called exorcists of His time: prayers, incantations, magic formulas, rituals, and even physical torture. He simply spoke with divine authority, and they obeyed, just as the winds and the waves had!

The demons made only one request: "Send us to the pigs; let us enter them" (v. 12). We are not told why the demons requested this, but Jesus granted it, a permission that then provided a vivid display of the Lord's power—a pig stampede. The panicked stampede of the pigs into the lake unveiled Satan's destructiveness. Why destroy what they requested for their refuge? Because that's what Satan does. Two thousand terrorized pigs stampeded to their watery grave. On the demons' part, it was an act of pure malice. They had nothing to gain but to delight in their destructiveness. Even pigs don't like demons! There is a significant insight here: Satan ultimately destroys whatever he touches, and so the demons find themselves deprived of the very thing they wanted: bodies!

We are not told what became of the demons. Since they are spiritual beings, they would not have perished with their hosts. Although we are not explicitly told, almost certainly they didn't have the freedom to inhabit other beings. As Mark Strauss wisely observes, "It is possible, of course, that they were now free to roam the earth and find other victims, but this is unlikely, since it would imply a win for them. Whenever Jesus encountered demons, they lose."[5]

When I was a college student, I wanted to hear the attacks of unbelievers on the gospel firsthand. One of the books I read was *Why I Am Not a Christian* by the well-known, aggressively agnostic philosopher Bertrand Russell. In the book, he cites this episode for his assertion that Jesus had serious defects in His moral character. As he writes, "It certainly was not very kind to the pigs to put devils into them and make them rush down the hill to the sea."[6] He neatly shifts the blame for the stampede to Jesus, but it wasn't the Lord who made the pigs rush into the sea; it was the demons. However, that stampede was a gift of grace to the people of the region; it enabled them to see that there was among them One who could set free even the most enslaved from the powers of darkness. That stampede summoned them to witness the miracle of transformation in the life of the notorious man they knew only too well. Animal rights have their place, but the Lord who taught that "you are of more value than many sparrows" (Matthew 10:31) considered that one oppressed man set free was worth more than two thousand pigs!

An Inescapable Choice of Kingdoms

The herdsmen fled and told it in the city and in the country. And people came to see what it was that had happened.

And they came to Jesus and saw the demon-possessed man, the one who had the legion, sitting there, clothed and in his right mind, and they were afraid. And those who had seen it described to them what had happened to the demon-possessed man and to the pigs. And they began to beg Jesus to depart from their region. As he was getting into the boat, the man who had been possessed with demons begged him that he might be with him. And he did not permit him but said to him, "Go home to your friends and tell them how much the Lord has done for you, and how he has had mercy on you." And he went away and began to proclaim in the Decapolis how much Jesus had done for him, and everyone marveled. (Mark 5:14–20)

People pay attention when their pocketbooks are affected. When the panicked herdsmen rushed into the village to describe what had happened to their pigs, crowds hurried out to see for themselves. It was both a curiosity and a catastrophe. It was certainly dramatic: pigs don't stampede into a lake. On the other hand, it was drastic: this large herd of pigs was probably the combined property of the entire village, and their loss had a terrible effect on the local economy. But what caught their attention when they reached the spot wasn't the absence of the pigs, but the presence of the man with Jesus, "sitting there, clothed and in his right mind" (v. 15). They knew from hard experience that this was entirely impossible. They had tried every possible means to control and tame the man, even using shackles and chains. All to no avail. But look at him now! The sight of the man, the absence of the pigs, and the realization that Jesus was responsible for these remarkable changes produced terror, rather than awe or even curiosity.

As the herdsmen recounted the events, the townspeople instantly decided they wanted nothing to do with Jesus: "They began to beg Jesus to depart from their region" (v. 17). Ironically, they had learned to live next door to pigs and even to a naked, demonized, violent man, but they had no intention of welcoming Jesus. Even though the Lord's power had been transforming in an amazingly positive way, they instinctively sensed that things would never be the same, were He to remain among them. They preferred the status quo.

I've seen a similar response in my world, when a person known for his broken life, perhaps marked by abusiveness and violence, comes to Christ. Often those who have been impacted the most by his past sinfulness react the most negatively to his conversion and changed life. Presented with the kingdom of light in the person of the Lord Jesus, these villagers chose the kingdom of darkness. They were every bit as much the prisoners of Satan as the demoniac had been.

The Lord Jesus honored their request. He would not force himself upon them. But as He was entering the boat, the ex-demoniac pleaded to be taken along with Him. He wanted all he could get of Jesus and more! But that was not part of the Lord's purpose for him. He was not to go with Jesus, but to go home to his friends and family, to present himself as Exhibit A of Jesus's transforming power, of "how much the Lord has done for you, and how he has had mercy on you" (v. 19). Jesus was sending him back into his world to be an agent of His kingdom and of the gospel. He was a man not only with a new life but with a new mission for it.

Mark entices us with the man's obedience: "And he went away and began to proclaim in the Decapolis how much Jesus had done for him, and everyone marveled" (v. 20). When we later read in Mark 7:31–37 about Jesus's return visit to this region of the Decapolis, we cannot help but wonder how many people came expectantly because they had heard about Him from the lips of this grateful man.

As the disciples entered the boat with Jesus to cross the lake to their home territory, they looked the same as they had on their arrival. But they weren't. On the lake, the Lord Jesus had taught them not to fear the powers of nature, but to live in awe of Him as the Lord of nature. On the far side of the lake, He had taught them not to fear the forces of evil or the forbidden ways of the Gentiles, but to trust Him as the One who is sovereign Lord over the domains of demons and of the Gentiles.

The disciples were learning more of Jesus so they could serve His mission more boldly and confidently in the world. And even a formerly demonized Gentile, who had experienced the liberating power of Jesus, had been enlisted for that mission. This miracle, like the previous one, calls us to live with a confidence in the Lord who brings freedom from fear. As our society is swept by strong tides of anti-Christian pressures, we need to fill our hearts with the greatness of who Jesus is. In that, we will be compelled to move forward to complete our mission, not to retreat in fear and self-protection. Jesus is the Lord of lords and the King of kings.

EIGHT

HELPLESS BUT NOT HOPELESS

On a recent New Year's Day, my wife and I found ourselves driving to the airport to pick up our college-age granddaughter from her time at a student missions conference. As we passed a certain exit, I suddenly remembered that exactly six years earlier I had been on that same highway, headed not for the airport but for the emergency room at the county hospital. Then, it was just minutes into the new year, and my adult daughter had been taken by ambulance from another hospital for expert follow-up after some troubling brain scans. Suddenly I found myself reliving the deep helplessness we felt when a resident appeared to tell us the tests revealed a tumor on her brain that would require surgery. I was her father. I had spent years of my life doing what I could to ward off or resolve the problems she encountered on her journey through life. But now I found myself utterly helpless to do anything that would make a difference, for either her or her two young children, who were blissfully asleep and unaware in their beds back at our home.

Helplessness is a terrible feeling, especially when it really matters. I can admit to feeling technologically helpless, but it is quite another thing when it is a life-and-death matter. And it is even worse when helplessness gets joined to hopelessness.

Helplessness and hopelessness come in many shapes and sizes. In the story we will consider in this chapter, we'll encounter two people who were different in almost every way. One was an influential and socially respectable man; the other, a sick and marginalized woman. But hardship and tragedy are the great levelers. The man found himself overwhelmed with desperation; the woman was locked in despair. That is precisely where the presence of Jesus made—and still makes—an incredible difference. Driven to Him because they had nowhere else to go, they discovered that faith in the Lord Jesus transforms everything.

During our time looking at the miracles of Jesus, we have found ourselves on and around the Sea of Galilee. At the end of Mark 4, we met the Lord and His disciples in a life-threatening storm out on the lake. Jesus commanded the winds and waters to calm, and they did. Then, on the eastern shore of the lake, in Gentile territory, they had encountered a man horribly dominated by demonic powers. At a word, the Lord set him free and restored him to himself. Both the forces of nature and the powers of darkness had bowed to the presence and power of the Lord Jesus. In every realm of life, Jesus is Lord.

That supremacy is once again on vivid display as we follow the Lord and His men back across the lake to His home territory of Capernaum, from which they had initially set out. Each of the synoptic gospel writers, Matthew, Mark, and Luke, records two intertwined miracle accounts. We will use Mark's account as our base, as Jesus reveals again that He is also Lord over disease and death.

The Public Agony of a Powerful Man

> And when Jesus had crossed again in the boat to the other side, a great crowd gathered about him, and he was beside the sea. Then came one of the rulers of the synagogue, Jairus by name, and seeing him, he fell at his feet and implored him earnestly, saying, "My little daughter is at the point of death. Come and lay your hands on her, so that she may be made well and live." And he went with him.
>
> And a great crowd followed him and thronged about him. (Mark 5:21–24)

We are not told how news of Jesus's return swept through Capernaum, but it obviously had. He was now the center of public attention, and although it is unlikely that reports of His encounter with the Gadarene demoniacs had already reached Capernaum, His return caused great excitement. Stepping onshore, He and His disciples were immediately surrounded by crowds of excited people. Some came to hear Him; even more, to see what astounding deed He might perform. But His miracles weren't acts of showmanship designed to attract a crowd or cause a sensation. Rather, they were signs of His true identity, foretastes of His kingdom, and illustrations of His message. All of those are evident in this remarkable passage.

Although the crowds were pushing against Jesus, they quickly gave way for a man determined to get to Jesus, a man instantly recognized by the gathered crowd. Jairus was a prominent man in Capernaum. Mark calls him "the synagogue ruler," while Matthew and Luke refer to him as "a ruler." Each of those titles indicates that he was a respected, influential member of society. "Synagogue ruler" was a prestigious role—a layperson elected to oversee synagogue affairs and organize Sabbath services. He was both a social and a spiritual leader, a man of high reputation and probably considerable wealth.

Jairus had obviously encountered Jesus before, since, as we have seen, Jesus was a regular participant in synagogue worship in Capernaum. He would therefore be familiar with both the Lord's miracles and His teaching, and almost certainly had participated in heated discussions about how the synagogue leaders ought to deal with Him. Jairus's natural alliances were with the scribes and Pharisees who viewed Jesus with alarm and anger. But now, those controversies must have seemed utterly irrelevant. He was facing an urgent problem: the imminent death of his beloved daughter. As a leader, he was used to solving problems. Now he could only watch with growing desperation as the life of his daughter slipped quickly away. She was only twelve, a young girl on the cusp of adulthood, and he was losing her.

Daughters get around their fathers' hearts in a special way. Every father can identify with the dread and desperation Jairus was feeling. My own daughter was in her forties when we faced the ugly reality of her diagnosis of an almost certainly fatal brain tumor. I can, in my own way, identify with Jairus. My daughter had two children, ages thirteen and seven, when she began her walk into the valley of the shadow of death. We, however, had an advantage that Jairus didn't have: we knew that Jesus is the Good Shepherd, who had conquered death and who never loses hold of any of His sheep.

Desperation drove Jairus to Jesus. Sacrificing his pride and perhaps even his reputation, setting aside the poise expected of such a man, and ignoring all the criticisms his religious associates would doubtless hurl at him, he flung himself at Jesus's feet in public agony. He didn't care about looking dignified or keeping up appearances; he cared only about his daughter.

There is an irony and insight here. The previous day, on the other side of the lake, a demonized, unclean Gentile had thrown himself at Jesus's feet. He had nowhere else to go to find relief from his demonic oppression. Now, on the other side of the lake, an orthodox, observant, and respected Jewish father found himself at those same feet. And so must we all, because salvation and hope can be found nowhere else.

As Jairus knelt before Jesus, he began to plead with a desperate faith that Jesus would come to heal his daughter. Jesus represented his only chance! And his faith was truly remarkable. All Jesus would need to do, he said, was to touch her, and she would be healed and live! He certainly showed no doubts about the Lord's power.

Without hesitation, Jesus agreed and set out for Jairus's home. By going with him, Jesus was, as it were, "taking the case," committing himself to do what He had been asked to do. He asked no questions of Jairus and established no conditions. He just went. The surrounding crowds suddenly became a spontaneous parade, following Jairus and Jesus. We can picture Jairus walking as fast as possible through the crowds, pushing people out of the way, accompanied by Jesus, with the disciples close behind. All the while, a growing crowd pressed to keep up, determined not to miss anything that might happen. They had no idea that this emergency run was about to come to a sudden halt.

The Private Agony of a Powerless Woman

> And there was a woman who had had a discharge of blood for twelve years, and who had suffered much under many physicians, and had spent all that she had, and was no better but rather grew worse. She had heard the reports about Jesus and came up behind him in the crowd and touched His garment. (Mark 5:25–27)

Unseen in the crowds pursuing Jesus was a woman who had been quietly biding her time, waiting for the right moment. She had no intention of interrupting Jesus or even talking to Him. Her plan was to remain anonymous, to do what she had come for, and then to melt quickly back into the crowd, unseen and unnoticed.

This woman was everything that Jairus wasn't. She was nameless, faceless, and marginalized, enduring a painfully personal but catastrophic and chronic medical problem. Her condition was debilitating enough—a persistent vaginal discharge that she had endured for years, an ailment that left her drained of energy. It had gone on for so long! In fact, she had been sick as long as Jairus's daughter had been alive—twelve long years.

Her condition was far more than a medical one. By the standards of the Mosaic law, a woman with a vaginal discharge was ceremonially unclean (Leviticus 15:19–30), a condition that affected everything she touched, spreading her uncleanness to people and things. This ritual uncleanness lasted for seven days in normal situations, and required extended purification rituals. But hers was not a normal menstrual situation. As a chronic condition, her ceremonial uncleanness was perpetual. So she found herself socially isolated and religiously excluded. In fact, she was virtually an untouchable, her social stigma similar in some ways to that of a leper. Were she married, her husband would have probably felt compelled to divorce her; if unmarried, she would have had no hope of marriage. Spiritually, she would also be an outsider, excluded from the temple and the local synagogue. And, in this woman's case, she had been impoverished by innumerable and useless medical treatments. She was the epitome of despair: powerless, ashamed, alone, poverty-stricken, and utterly hopeless.

However, reports of Jesus's remarkable healings had ignited within her a tiny spark of hope. News of Jesus's return had inspired a plan, and the abrupt parade had provided a unique opportunity. It was risky to even be in the crowd—were she recognized she would be not only deeply shamed but also in grave danger. But the crowd also provided an opportunity! Her plan was to "touch and go." It would all be completely secret. No one need ever know, perhaps not even Jesus. She would inch close to Him in the crowd, touch Him slightly, then quietly melt back into the sea of people. That, she believed, was all it would take. She would be made well. And, if she wasn't, what had she lost by the attempt? But she had no doubts: Jesus could do this. And so, she stealthily pushed closer to carry out her plan.

From Helpless to Healthy and Hopeful: Jesus and the Woman

> And immediately the flow of blood dried up, and she felt in her body that she was healed of her disease. And Jesus, perceiving in himself that power had gone out from him, immediately turned about in the crowd and said, "Who touched my garments?" And his disciples said to him, "You see the crowd pressing around you, and yet you say, 'Who touched me?'" And he looked around to see who had done it. But the woman, knowing what had happened to her, came in fear and trembling and fell down before him and told him the whole truth. And he said to her, "Daughter, your faith has made you well; go in peace, and be healed of your disease." (Mark 5:29–34)

She touched Him! Well, not Him exactly. Matthew and Luke tell us that she touched the fringe of His garment, perhaps just the hem or the tassels that hung from a Jewish man's robes. Even He couldn't possibly feel such a touch, she must have thought, especially with so many people jostling against Him in a surging crowd. Having faith to believe she could be healed just by touching Jesus's clothing may seem almost magical and superstitious, but it was real.

So was what happened next. She felt it to the depths of her body. Something had changed. She knew she had been healed! Joyful as she felt, she knew she couldn't show her elation with a shout of joy or even an excited laugh. Quietly, carefully, she melted back into the crowd, hiding until she could get away. She had received what she had come for—a cure! Jesus had done for her what no else could.

But her getaway plans didn't go quite as she planned. Jesus suddenly stopped, saying loudly enough for all to hear, "Who touched me?" (v. 31). His words raise many questions. Had healing power flowed from Jesus almost impersonally, without His consent? This is the only healing Jesus performed that wasn't at His direct initiative. Was His power simply an impersonal force, like an electric current, that can just be plugged into? Did He really not know the recipient? Those might be valid interpretations, if we didn't have so many other examples of Jesus's miracles. His power was personal, not impersonal; His healings were intentional, not accidental. It is far more likely that Jesus did know whom He had healed and how. His question was intended to force this poor woman to reveal herself to Him, because, although she did not know it, He had more to do for her. He intended His healing to go far deeper than her body. Her physical healing was significant, but not sufficient. Her wounded soul needed healing as deeply as her broken body had.

The disciples were incredulous that Jesus would stop and ask such an apparently foolish thing. After all, they were on an emergency mission. A girl was dying, and time was short. What difference did it make if someone had touched Him? Luke tells us, "When all denied it, Peter said, 'Master, the crowds surround you and are pressing in on you'" (Luke 8:45). The other gospels make it clear that Peter was not alone in his frustration with Jesus. It is remarkable how persistent the disciples, especially Peter, were in their self-deceived notion that Jesus needed the benefit of their advice. But a moment's honest introspection reminds us that we are often all too sure of how the Lord Jesus should act in any given situation.

Jesus would not be put off. He insisted on staying where He was until the healed person revealed herself. Jesus wasn't interested in dispensing "bump and run" solutions. His intention was not merely to make sick people better; He wanted to make broken people whole.

The woman realized that if the Lord knew about her touch, He must also know about her identity. She knew she couldn't stay hidden. Perhaps she also had a fear of Jesus's awesome power. If she didn't reveal herself would He act against her? So, in fear and trembling, she pushed forward, threw herself at the feet of Jesus, and blurted out her confession. She was the toucher! But she also finished the story of "how she had been immediately healed" (Luke 8:47).

She had nothing to fear. Jesus's words to her were not words of rebuke but of compassion and healing. A woman who had suffered in secret was now brought into the light of grace: "Daughter, your faith has made you well; go in peace, and be healed of your disease" (Mark 5:34). It was faith in Jesus, not a superstitious touch, that had healed her. She had been healed because she trusted Him, not just because she had touched Him. In addition to this story, there are three other times in the Gospels when Jesus declared a person's faith had made them well or saved them (Mark 10:52; Luke 7:50; 17:19). Two things should be noticed. First, the faith in view each time is faith in Jesus. It reminds us of a fundamental principle: we are made right with God on the basis of who God is and what He has done in the person and work of the Lord Jesus Christ. Faith in Jesus—trust in His death for our sins and His risen life and power—is the means by which God delivers us from the guilt and penalty of sin. Faith is not the basis of our salvation; Jesus is. But faith, not our works, personal achievements, or religious activities, is the agent by which we lay hold of God's provision. Saving faith is not merely a belief in the right things, but active trust in the Lord himself.

Second, while the statement "Your faith has made you well" could simply mean, "Your faith [in Me] has led to your healing," it almost certainly means far more. The Lord used a very particular expression—"your faith *has* made you well," not "your faith healed you." (For grammarians, past perfect rather than simple past tense.) The Lord is stressing the certainty and the permanence of her healing, a healing that enables her to live in God's peace. To "go in peace," as the Lord commands, is a declaration that she has been made whole. It is a Hebrew blessing that describes her restoration to God. She had been released from a terrible illness. Now, by this declaration in front of the crowds, the Lord was releasing her from the social stigma she had endured for so many years. And by His blessing of peace, He is assuring her of her right standing before God himself.

From Death to Life: Jesus, Jairus, and Resurrection Power

> While he was still speaking, there came from the ruler's house some who said, "Your daughter is dead. Why trouble the Teacher any further?" But overhearing what they said, Jesus said to the ruler of the synagogue, "Do not fear, only believe." And he allowed no one to follow him except Peter and James and John the brother of James. They came to the house of the ruler of the synagogue, and Jesus saw a commotion, people weeping and wailing loudly. And when he had entered, he said to them, "Why are you making a commotion and weeping? The child is not dead but sleeping." And they laughed at him. But he put them all outside and

took the child's father and mother and those who were with him and went in where the child was. Taking her by the hand he said to her, "Talitha cumi," which means, "Little girl, I say to you, arise." And immediately the girl got up and began walking (for she was twelve years of age), and they were immediately overcome with amazement. And he strictly charged them that no one should know this, and told them to give her something to eat. (Mark 5:35–43)

I don't imagine Jairus enjoyed Jesus's encounter with the woman who touched his clothing to be healed. How could Jesus dally when his daughter was dying? Time was the enemy, and it was ticking away. This woman was a nobody, who had been sick for twelve years. A few minutes here or there wouldn't matter to her or change her condition. But his twelve-year-old daughter was dying! He must have been thinking what the disciples had asked during the storm: "Why are you sleeping? Don't you care that we're perishing?" From Jairus's perspective, Jesus's delay was a denial.

What Jairus did not, and could not, have known was that time had already run out for his daughter. Then, while Jesus was still engaged with this woman, he was forced to face the unthinkable: his daughter was already dead. A messenger arrived from the family, bringing the heartbreaking news. There was, the messenger told him, no need to bother Jesus any longer. The worst had happened. The time for hope had gone; now was the time for grief. After hearing how the messenger spoke of Jairus "troubling" Jesus and seeing the response of those present when Jesus and Jairus finally reached his home, I wonder if the rest of the family viewed Jairus's trust in Jesus's ability to heal as an act of desperate foolishness?

The Lord interrupted the messenger's report with a strong and compassion-filled challenge: "Do not fear; only believe" (Mark 5:36). Luke adds a promise: "and she will be well" (8:50). The assertion must have seemed patently ridiculous. Dead daughters don't get well. Jairus had no reason to doubt that the report of her death was true. But then again, standing in front of him was visible proof of the power of Jesus. Perhaps the healing of the woman had been divinely arranged to bolster Jairus's faith in Jesus at that very moment. The Lord Jesus was giving a promise: "It's not over, even though it looks like it is." So, perhaps with a glance back at the woman, Jairus strode quickly toward his home, accompanied by Jesus and His special trio of disciples, Peter, James, and John. What was about to happen was a "must see" moment for them.

Upon their arrival, they entered a scene of pandemonium and despair: "a commotion, people weeping and wailing loudly" (Mark 5:38). Middle Eastern tradition does not encounter death with the stoicism and hushed tones typical of modern Westerners. Our grief is somber and quiet. Middle Eastern and Jewish grief was loud, flamboyant, physical, and public. In fact, later rabbis would require professional mourners and flute players so that people could do their grieving properly.[1] But we should not misunderstand. This grief was not in any way contrived. It was real, deep, and heartrending.

There was probably a moment of hushed silence when Jairus entered the house with Jesus. And the Lord's first statement was, to say the least, startling: "Why are you making a commotion and weeping? The child is not dead but sleeping" (v. 39). No wonder they responded with contemptuous laughter! It felt like He was mocking their grief. There was no doubt that the girl was dead. These people knew the difference between life and death, because they lived much closer to death than we do, in our anesthetized and antiseptic world. Death was no stranger to them. To say the least, Jesus's words were cryptic. He was declaring that her condition, terminal though it was, was not permanent. In His presence, it would only be temporary.

Then Jesus took charge of the situation. Putting everyone else out of the house except the girl's parents and His disciples, He went to the cot where the girl's body lay. Taking her hand, He spoke two words, a phrase so memorable that it seems Peter must have recounted the Aramaic words to Mark, "Talitha cumi," or "Little girl, I say to you, arise" (v. 41).[2] These were words that Jairus had probably used to awaken his sleeping daughter over the years. As we've seen before, there was no prolonged prayer, no magical words, no extended ritual. The Lord Jesus simply spoke two words, and to the utter amazement of all those present in the room, "immediately the girl got up and began walking." The atmosphere in the room must have been electric: incredible joy, profound astonishment, deep wonder, and even an element of fear. Mark simply declares they were "overcome with amazement" (v. 42).

Jesus is Lord over life and death. Three times in the Gospels He restores a dead person to life—this daughter of Jairus, the son of a widow in the Galilean town of Nain (Luke 7:11–17), and Lazarus, the brother of Martha and Mary (John 11). Each of these "restorations" would have been followed by the later death of that person, but each pointed to the resurrection of the Lord Jesus into a body that would never again die. The supreme miracle of the resurrection of the Lord Jesus forms the solid foundation upon which our hope rests. One day, when He returns, we will receive our resurrection bodies.

The story ends abruptly with the Lord's charge not to tell anyone what had happened. Did He really expect them to keep this quiet? How could they? A dead girl was alive! More likely, He wanted them to restrain themselves for a time, allowing Jesus and His disciples to get away from the area, preventing a hysterical mob response. He was guarding against sensationalism. The focus of His ministry was not on His miracles, great as they are, but on His message.

The miracles that we have considered in the last three chapters have given us a remarkable picture of the power and authority of the Lord Jesus Christ. On Lake Galilee, with a single word, He demonstrated His power over the winds and the waves, the powers of nature. On the far side of the lake, by the power of His word, He forced a legion of demonic powers of darkness to submit to His authority. Back on home soil, a woman held by the power of disease was healed without a word, and then Jesus's word of blessing healed her soul as well. And with two words spoken to Jairus's daughter, He broke the power of death. Nature. Demons. Disease. Death. He is Lord of all.

We have also seen His compassion reaching in all directions: to His disciples; a demonized pagan; a disease-broken, poverty-stricken woman; and a prestigious, influential, but despairing member of the elite. Each needed the Lord in a very personal way. Each realized they had nowhere else to go. But when they turned to Jesus and trusted Him, they experienced His saving, healing power. They found themselves in positions of helplessness. But helplessness isn't hopelessness in the presence of the Lord Jesus. When life seems to give us no place to go, the only place to go is to Him.

NINE

LORD OF THE SUFFERER AND THE SABBATH

On New Year's Day in 2019, a new law went into effect in New York City, enabling adults to change the gender on their own birth certificates from M or F to X, if they so desire. No medical documentation is required. Parents of newborns could also choose X for the gender of their baby. When Mayor Bill DeBlasio signed the bill after the city council passed it, he celebrated with the declaration: "You be you. Live your truth. Know that New York City will have your back."[1]

It was a classic expression of the prevailing cultural value of what has been called "expressive individualism" or "radical autonomy." One of its major proponents has described it as "a desire to pursue one's own path. . . , a yearning for fulfillment through the definition and articulation of one's own identity. It is a drive to be more like you already are. . . . The capacity of individuals to define the terms of their own existence . . . is given pride of place in our self-understanding."[2] Or to put it in the slogans we hear so often: "Follow your heart!" "Find your freedom!" "Live your own truth!"

Christ-followers live by entirely different principles: "Follow your Lord." "Find His freedom." "Live by God's truth." The goal in life isn't to find ourselves, but to find and follow the Lord Jesus, because, when we do, we find not only our true identity but true freedom as well. As the Lord declared, "If the Son sets you free, you will be free indeed" (John 8:36).

But why trust Him, rather than myself or the prevailing ideas of our culture? In a postmodern world, it is fashionable to say that all claims to truth are equally valid and deserve our respect. But, deep down, no one really believes that. Some beliefs are foolish. Others are dangerous. How can we tell the difference?

That is one of the reasons we pay attention to the miracles Jesus performed, especially His resurrection. They bring us into direct contact with the One who is absolute truth. The story in this chapter brings us not only a remarkable miracle of the Lord but also a stunning claim by Him. If what He says is true, it changes everything. The miracle and the claim marked a major turning point in the ministry of Jesus. It may not have been as spectacular to see as some others, but it led to one of Jesus's most profound declarations about who He is. The result was a controversy that split public opinion and set in motion events that led inevitably to His crucifixion.

The Problem at the Pool: "The House of Misery"

> After this there was a feast of the Jews, and Jesus went up to Jerusalem.
> Now there is in Jerusalem by the Sheep Gate a pool, in Aramaic called Bethesda, which has five roofed colonnades. In these lay a multitude of invalids—blind, lame, and paralyzed. (John 5:1–3)

The miracles of the Lord Jesus we have considered so far have all taken place in and around Lake Galilee. Now the scene shifts to Jerusalem. He had been there before and done numerous miracles there, although none of them are recorded in the Gospels. John tells us in John 2:23 that "when he was in Jerusalem at the Passover Feast, many believed in his name when they saw the signs that he was doing." When the eminent Pharisee Nicodemus came to interview Jesus at night, he began the conversation with the words, "Rabbi, we know that you are a teacher come from God, for no one can do these signs that you do unless God is with him" (John 3:2). So the Lord had done numerous miracles in Jerusalem, and they had aroused both curiosity and controversy about Him. Now, with the miracle He was about to perform, those whispered questions would become a roaring debate. Stirring up that debate was undoubtedly one of the reasons Jesus did what He did, and why He chose this particular place and time. Nothing was happening by chance.

God's law, given through Moses in the Torah, required Jewish men to travel to the place God had set apart for sacrifice three times a year. At this point in Israel's history, that place was the temple in Jerusalem, and the three pilgrim festivals were Passover, Pentecost, and Tabernacles. This miracle, John tells us, took place during one of those feasts, but he doesn't deem it necessary to tell us which one. Speculation is therefore both unnecessary and unhelpful.

We do know, however, that a feast was a time when Jerusalem's population would triple or quadruple. The walled city would be jammed with tens of thousands of Jewish worshippers, coming from all over the country, as well as from distant lands. The streets would become a beehive of activity, centering on the magnificent temple complex. Built by Herod the Great, it was one of the architectural wonders of the world in its day. To the northeast of the city, just outside the city walls, there was another structure known as the pool of Bethesda. John tells us that it was by "the Sheep Gate" (John 5:2), the gate through which the sacrificial animals would be brought into the city. The pool itself was a large reservoir about three hundred feet long. There were, in fact, two pools surrounded by four covered porches, with a fifth porch separating the two. For centuries, John was accused of making a mistake in saying such a pool even existed, but John was proven correct when the pools were uncovered in 1888, during a renovation of the nearby Church of St. Anne.

Water entered the pools by aqueduct and was collected in the limestone structure, and there may have also been some underground springs that were intermittently active. For whatever reason, volumes of water would occasionally erupt, stirring up the water throughout the entire pool. It seems a superstition arose that this movement in the water was caused by an angel stirring the water, and that the first person into the pool after this eruption occurred would be healed. Such ideas were not uncommon in the ancient world, and portions of the Jewish population were not exempt from adopting such superstitions. It is intriguing that, after the Romans destroyed the temple, they later built a shrine on this very site, dedicated to Asclepius, their god of healing. So the local superstition outlasted the temple!

The belief that the waters had miraculous power was like a magnet to desperately ill people. Dozens, and perhaps hundreds, had been drawn to the pool, both by the hope of healing and also by the shade the porches provided in the brutal heat of the Judean sun. There is irony here: Bethesda means "house of mercy," but the place was in fact "a house of misery." The sense of hopelessness would have been almost tangible, and the stench due to a lack of sanitation would have been overwhelming. A crowd of largely immobile people would hardly be able to care properly for their bodily needs.

The entire scene made this a disreputable place, closer to a homeless encampment than an overcrowded emergency room. This was not on anyone's "must see" list of places to go in Jerusalem. The folk religion and superstition was dishonoring to God, and the uncleanness could contaminate visitors, rendering them ceremonially unclean for temple worship. This was a place the orthodox and the well-to-do chose to avoid. But Jesus went there, and almost certainly took His disciples with Him. When you follow Jesus, you may end up in some very unexpected places!

Lord of the Sufferer: "Do You Want to Be Healed?"

> One man was there who had been an invalid for thirty-eight years. When Jesus saw him lying there and knew that he had already been there a long time, he said to him, "Do you want to be healed?" The sick man answered him, "Sir, I have no one to put me into the pool when the water is stirred up, and while I am going another steps down before me." Jesus said to him, "Get up, take up your bed, and walk." And at once the man was healed, and he took up his bed and walked. (John 5:5–9)

When He entered the pool area, the Lord Jesus found himself surrounded by an ocean of human need. For reasons known only to Him, He focused His attention on just one man. We aren't given the exact nature of his illness, although he seems to have been immobile, or nearly so, due to paralysis or a debilitating illness. It wasn't the product of age—he had been like that for perhaps his entire adult life—thirty-eight long years! By now, he was the epitome of helplessness and hopelessness. His body was present, but his hope had long since vanished. Hardened and embittered, he had become a crotchety old man who saw himself only as a victim.

Perhaps it was because he was so helpless that Jesus singled him out. Curiosity presses the question on us: Why him? It wasn't his potential. Most of his life had already passed. Most of the others present would have been much younger than him. It certainly wasn't his winsome personality or charm. I think he's one of the most unattractive people we meet in the Gospels. His face would appropriately illustrate the word "curmudgeon" in an illustrated dictionary. And it wasn't his faith; he doesn't even seem to know who Jesus is.

Yet this is the man toward whom Jesus moved. For reasons hidden in His own heart and His sovereign purpose, Jesus chose to intervene in his life. The Lord doesn't have to explain His grace; He is free to bestow it wherever He desires. In fact, the very reason Jesus may have been drawn to this man was that he obviously had nothing to offer but his need. He was truly hopeless. If Jesus could do something for this man, He could do something for anyone.

If the Lord's choice of this man is unexpected, the Lord's first words are even more so: "Do you want to be healed?" (v. 6). The question jars our ears. Of course he wants to get better; who wouldn't? But while I may be prone to asking foolish questions, the Lord isn't.

The Lord was carefully probing the man's soul. A little experience dealing with people teaches us we can become wedded to our problems, constantly rehearsing them to all who will listen, but never arousing the energy to do what is required to change the situation or our attitude toward it. In the midst of marriage counseling, I have asked the question, "Do you want this to get better?" and had a woman vehemently respond, "I'd rather stay angry at him." Struggling with addictions to alcohol, drugs, or pornography, the question arises, "Do you want to get better or just to feel better?"

The man apparently had no idea who was speaking to him, but his response was telling. He didn't answer the question: "Of course I do." Instead, he launched into his oft-repeated lament: "Sir, I have no one to put me into the pool when the water is stirred up, and while I am going another steps down before me" (v. 7). But Jesus hadn't asked him whether he wanted to get wet; He had asked him whether he wanted to get well. Clearly this is a man who had resigned himself to his lot in life, having given up all hope. And yet he had arranged for someone to keep bringing him back to the pool. He may not have liked his condition, but he had come to terms with it. Perhaps he was even trying to recruit Jesus to be his helper!

But Jesus didn't turn His back on this faithless, hopeless man. Instead, He suddenly gave a sharp command: "Get up, take up your bed [better, 'mat'], and walk" (v. 8).

As before, there was no intermediate agency, no incantation of a special formula, not even a petition to His heavenly Father. There was just an emphatic command for the man to do what he knew he couldn't do—get up and walk.

Amazingly the man did just that. He tried to get up and succeeded! Why did he even try? The only explanation must be that the Lord who commanded the impossible enabled the impossible. The man must have felt something happen in his broken body, and even though he didn't know who was commanding him to get up, somehow he instinctively knew that he could, and should, do what this anonymous figure had told him to do. The healing was instant and complete: "At once the man was healed, and he took up his bed and walked" (v. 9).

We should not miss the completeness of his healing. Not only was his paralysis erased; thirty-eight years of muscle deterioration from immobility was instantly reversed. His ability to pick up and carry that little mat was public evidence of the completeness of his healing.

We are told nothing of the reaction of either the man or the crowds around the pool, but there must have been an outbreak of astonished celebration. Carrying the little mat on which he had spent so much of his life was proof of his remarkable and unexplainable transformation. His time at the pool was over. With all the jubilation capturing the crowd's attention, Jesus slipped quietly away, without even a word of gratitude from the healed man. After a time, the healed man headed away from the pool, carrying his mat over his shoulder, little realizing that the visible symbol of his new life was about to become a red flag waving in the face of some theological bulls.

Lord of the Sabbath: "Making Himself Equal with God"

> Now that day was the Sabbath. So the Jews said to the man who had been healed, "It is the Sabbath, and it is not lawful for you to take up your bed." But he answered them, "The man who healed me, that man said to me, 'Take up your bed, and walk.'" They asked him, "Who is the man who said to you, 'Take up your bed and walk'?" Now the man who had been healed did not know who it was, for Jesus had withdrawn, as there was a crowd in the place. Afterward Jesus found him in the temple and said to him, "See, you are well! Sin no more, that nothing worse may happen to you." The man went away and told the Jews that it was Jesus who had healed him. And this was why the Jews were persecuting Jesus, because he was doing these things on the Sabbath. But Jesus answered them, "My Father is working until now, and I am working."
>
> This was why the Jews were seeking all the more to kill him, because not only was he breaking the Sabbath, but he was even calling God his own Father, making himself equal with God. (John 5:9–18)

It is remarkable how a simple sentence can change everything: "Now that day was the Sabbath." John has skillfully concealed that fact from us until this moment, as the healed man carried his mat through Jerusalem, perhaps heading to the temple for the first time in almost forty years. To understand what happened next, we need to understand what the Sabbath had come to mean in first-century Judaism.

There were many things that set the Jewish people apart from the people of other nations. But three things had pride of place as identity markers: the Sabbath, strict adherence to Jewish food laws, and circumcision as a sign of their covenant with God through Abraham. Each set them apart in its own way, but the Sabbath perhaps most of all. It was, of course, a divine command contained in the Ten Commandments (Exodus 20:8–10), as a specific sign for them as a nation (Exodus 31:13, 16–17). In fact, the Sabbath had become, for the Jewish religious leaders, the supreme identity marker. As the rabbis would later say, "The Sabbath outweighs all the commandments of the Torah."[3]

To protect against violation of the Sabbath, Jewish tradition had developed an elaborate system of man-made regulations to put a fence around the Sabbath. Obviously, you were not to work on the Sabbath, but what constituted work?

When some Jewish leaders, likely Pharisees, saw a man blatantly carrying a mat, they were compelled to stop and question him. They told him, "It is not lawful for you to take up your bed" (John 5:10). There is no law in the Torah concerning carrying a burden. However, God had spoken directly about the matter through Jeremiah:

Thus said the LORD to me: "Go and stand in the People's Gate, by which the kings of Judah enter and by which they go out, and in all the gates of Jerusalem, and say: 'Hear the word of the LORD, you kings of Judah, and all Judah, and all the inhabitants of Jerusalem, who enter by these gates. Thus says the LORD: Take care for the sake of your lives, and do not bear a burden on the Sabbath day or bring it in by the gates of Jerusalem. And do not carry a burden out of your houses on the Sabbath or do any work, but keep the Sabbath day holy, as I commanded your fathers.' " (Jeremiah 17:19–22)

Here was a man clearly in violation of God's declared will!

It was not by accident that the Lord Jesus chose to heal this man and to command him to carry his mat on a Sabbath day. The man had been immobile for thirty-eight years—what difference would it have made if Jesus had done it the next day? No. Jesus deliberately healed on the Sabbath. And this wasn't Jesus's only Sabbath miracle. In fact, it seems almost to have been a deliberate policy—the Gospels record Him performing at least seven miracles on the Sabbath.[4] While the rabbis had some inclination to accept healings on the Sabbath, were the situation life-threatening, this miracle clearly didn't fall into that category. Jesus's act was intended to do more than bring relief to a hurting man; it was designed to provoke a response from His theological opponents. He was making an enormous claim about His identity. If the healing of the man at the pool had exposed the shallowness of popular superstitions, the healing of the man on the Sabbath was exposing the heartlessness of religious legalists and the blindness of theological rigorists who had become wedded to man-made traditions.

If Jesus had intended to provoke controversy, He was obviously successful. Before the healed man had traveled very far, mat in hand, he found himself surrounded by some theological police demanding that he account for his outrageous behavior. John records the aftermath of the miracle in a series of four brief scenes that lead to one of the great chapters in the New Testament, as throughout the rest of chapter 5, the Lord debates and declares His true identity as one with God His Father to the Jewish leaders. Sadly, both our present purpose and space prevent us from fully engaging that debate, but John's introduction to it gives us much to ponder.

The first scene involves the challenge of the mat-carrying healed man by a band of Jewish authorities. There was no debate about the facts of the case: "It is the Sabbath, and it is not lawful for you to take up your bed" (John 5:10). All the man could do in response was to blurt out an account of what had happened: a man had healed him and had told him to pick up his bed and walk. Perhaps he expected them to recognize that a man who could heal a paralyzed man was a man who was to be obeyed. After all, in the Old Testament, it was God's great prophets, men like Elijah and Elisha, who had done such miracles. But the leaders had no interest in the man's explanation. What was tragically apparent is that these men had absolutely no interest in this man or the remarkable thing that had happened to him. They had no joy or even curiosity about a paralyzed man walking on his own. All that mattered to them was the violation of their cherished religious rules. Their only question was about the identity of the miracle-worker. They did not deny the reality of the miracle. They could not. Sadly, their traditions had hardened their hearts and blinded their eyes to God's truth. The man can't answer their questions. He had been so taken up first with his own complaints and then with his remarkable healing that he had failed to even learn who had transformed his life.

Sometime later a second scene took place. Despite the throngs filling the temple courts, Jesus found the man and gave him both a greeting and a warning: "See, you are well! Sin no more, that nothing worse may happen to you" (v. 14). He wanted the man to have answers for the Jewish leaders' questions. His cryptic warning about sin has puzzled many Bible readers, but it seems to suggest that the man's earlier disability was the consequence of some sin in which he had been engaged. It is perilous to speculate further, and we must remember that the Lord had insights into the man that we don't have. In fact, in John 9, as we will see, the Lord makes it very clear that another man's blindness was in no way related to his sin. I've known too many who are convinced that every sin or sickness can be connected to a particular issue of sin. On that basis, they often try to force a person to confess their sickness-producing sin, which only increases their suffering. The Lord knew about this man, as He knows about all people. Contemporary sin-inspectors don't have such insight and are often blind to many of their own sins.

The encounter between the Lord and the healed man had a sad ending. There is no indication that the man thanked Jesus, fell down before Him in grateful worship, or confessed faith in Him. His legs had been healed, but not his heart. His immediate re-sponse was to rush to the temple watch guards in order to clear himself of breaking the Sabbath regulations by informing on Jesus. He was willing to betray Jesus to minimize trouble for himself. And with that, this unattractive man vanished from the scene.

Now the Jewish leaders had Jesus squarely in their sights. Prob-ably His identity was no surprise—who else could have done such an act? The One who had troubled them before was doing it once again. But this time, they had clear ammunition against Him. He was a Sabbath-breaker, a threat to the established order of things. He was guilty of the crime of breaking God's law (as they had chosen to understand it): That, says John, "was why the Jews were persecuting Jesus, because he was doing these things on the Sabbath" (v. 16).

Blatant Sabbath violation would have been enough to inspire their campaign against Him, but Jesus escalated the conflict with a remarkable claim: "My Father is working until now, and I am work-ing" (v. 17). To understand this in connection with the Sabbath, we need to realize that the rabbis understood that the Sabbath law didn't apply to God. He was free to act on the Sabbath—after all, He continued to sustain and rule all creation, even on the seventh day. There was a Sabbath exemption for God. The Lord Jesus was claiming that "Sabbath God-exemption" for himself!

By healing on the Sabbath, Jesus was claiming the same right to supersede the Sabbath that God himself has. Furthermore, He spoke of God as His Father. We need to realize that Judaism by this time had virtually ceased using the divine name *Yahweh*, by which God had revealed himself to Moses in Exodus 3:16. (Nearly all our English Bibles carry on this tradition by rendering the Hebrew YHWH as "Lord.") Even today, observant Jews will speak of God as *HaShem*, "the Name," so as to avoid any blasphemous familiarity with God by speaking His name. But Jesus was going much further. He was referring to YHWH God Almighty as "my Father." By healing on the Sabbath, He was claiming divine prerogatives. By referring to God as His "Father," He was "making himself equal with God" (John 5:18).

Our ears don't hear the scandal of that, because we have been taught by the Lord Jesus to speak of God as our Father. But in the Old Testament, while God is referred to as the Father of the nation of Israel, the title "Father" occurs only nine times. Never does an individual speak of God as "my Father." In contrast, it is true to say that "Father" is the Christian name for God. That is because, through the Lord Jesus, God's Son, we have been adopted into the family of God and given an entirely new relationship with God.

In the rest of John 5, Jesus will reinforce His astonishing claims to have the rights and entitlements of God and to speak to God as His Father, in ways transcending mere metaphor. In earlier chapters, by His words and miracles the Lord Jesus showed himself to be Lord over nature, Lord over the demonic realm, Lord over disease, and Lord over death itself. Now we hear Him declaring not only that He is Lord over disability but that He is Lord over the Sabbath instituted by God himself.

He has the same relation to the Sabbath as His Father does. In the dialogue that follows in John 5, He will declare that He is able to do whatever the Father does (5:19). He possesses resurrection power, and gives life to the dead (5:21). He is the final Judge, who determines the destiny of all His creatures (5:23–24). He is the Savior, who gives eternal life to all who believe in Him (5:24). He is one with God.

All that Jesus said and did was so that we might understand who He is. And the wonder is this: the One who sees and heals a broken, cantankerous disabled man is the Lord of glory, God the Son, the eternal God, the final Judge. He became human and went to the cross so that everyone who trusts Him and the Father who sent Him "does not come into judgment, but has passed from death to life" (John 5:24). Before Him we rightly fall in worship, as Thomas did, declaring, "My Lord and my God!" (John 20:28).

TEN

MORE THAN ENOUGH

About a hundred years ago, a Scottish preacher named George Morrison wrote a sermon entitled "Peace, the Possession of Adequate Resources." It is an idea that often comes to my mind. I vividly recall times, years ago, when our family would make long trips by car. More than once, I found myself driving on a lonely, unfamiliar stretch of highway in the early hours of the morning with my wife and children fast asleep. This was a time long before Google Maps, and as my gas gauge moved lower and lower, my anxiety steadily rose higher and higher. I had no idea when the next gas station would appear over the horizon. Visions of being stranded in the middle of nowhere would fill my mind, and my petitions to the Lord grew more fervent. Then, wonderfully, as the need was becoming urgent, I would happen upon an open station. The road was no less desolate and unfamiliar on the other side of that station, but my now full tank of gas made all the difference to my peace of mind.

There have been many similar times: when tuition payments were due or our car began making ominous noises and our bank account was already perilously low; when the market took a sharp downward turn, and our preparation for retirement was threatened; when medical bills loomed.

But it isn't only in the realm of finances that we need adequate resources. In my pastoral ministry, there have been many times I've felt an overwhelming sense of inadequacy: my first funeral; visiting a grieving parent after the sudden death of a child; having to tell a young wife and mother that her husband had been murdered; dealing with church crises of various kinds. I knew I was out of my depth and needed more than I could bring to the table.

Probably I've felt it most in my family life: when my bride and I headed off into another country and an unclear future, feeling the new weight of responsibility; holding my newborn daughter, feeling an even greater responsibility; when, decades later, I brought that same but now terminally ill daughter back into our home so she could spend her last days in a place where she would be loved, sheltered, and cared for; when my wife was diagnosed with breast cancer. Who is sufficient for these things? Not me—but I needed to be.

Your list would be similar, but distinctly yours. Reality is the same for all of us, young or old, rich or poor, single or married. Whatever our situation in life, circumstances often push us beyond our competency and comfort zones. Honest people are driven to the humble recognition that they don't have all it takes, no matter how loudly the positive thinkers trumpet, "You can do anything you set your mind to!" Perhaps that is why the Lord's miracle of feeding the five thousand is not only one of His best-known miracles but one of His most beloved.

Apparently the gospel writers felt the same way because this is the only miracle of Jesus described in all four gospels (with the exception, of course, of His resurrection). It is a miracle that tells us in a powerful way that the Lord Jesus is not only superior; He is sufficient. He is not only enough; He is necessary.

Each of the gospel writers describes this miracle from a unique perspective, emphasizing aspects that were of particular importance to his presentation of Jesus. This is hardly surprising—each of us would describe an event that we shared with others in a particular way, even though we wouldn't completely agree on the specifics. We have the privilege of reading all four accounts, so while we will view this event primarily through the eyes of John, who was an active participant in it, we will also make use of information from the other gospels.

An Interrupted Retreat: When Life Interrupts Our Plans

> After this Jesus went away to the other side of the Sea of Galilee, which is the Sea of Tiberias. And a large crowd was following him, because they saw the signs that he was doing on the sick. Jesus went up on the mountain, and there he sat down with his disciples. Now the Passover, the feast of the Jews, was at hand. (John 6:1–4)

In our previous chapter, we looked at John 5 and saw Jesus engaged in a controversy with the Jewish leaders because He healed a disabled man at the pool of Bethesda on a Sabbath day. Now, as John begins his next chapter, he rather abruptly tells us that Jesus is back in Galilee, making His way by boat from His home area of Capernaum to the northeastern shore of Lake Galilee. Helpfully, the other three gospels help us to fill in the backstory of this momentous event.

After the events recorded in John 5, the Lord had returned to Galilee to continue His itinerant ministry of teaching and healing. His popularity had only increased in His absence, perhaps accelerated by reports from other pilgrims who had also been in Jerusalem during the feast. But two other things of importance have taken place as we enter this story.

The first is that the Lord Jesus had commissioned His disciples to venture out on preaching missions of their own throughout Galilee. He had not only charged them to preach His message of God's kingdom but He had also empowered them to do miracles in His name. They went and did what He had done—teach, cast out demons, and heal (Mark 6:12–13; Luke 9:6).

At the same time, events related to John the Baptist, the Lord's forerunner, had taken a dark turn. The Baptist had become increasingly vocal in his denouncements of Herod Antipas, the ruler in Galilee. Finally, in a total miscarriage of justice, Herod reacted by having John imprisoned, and then beheaded (Matthew 14:1–12; Mark 6:14–29). Given John's massive popularity, this was a nation-shaking event.

The two events converged, when the disciples returned at almost the same time that reports of John's judicial murder reached Jesus. So, while the disciples were excitedly telling Jesus "all that they had done and taught" (Mark 6:30), John's disciples "went and told Jesus" about his execution (Matthew 14:12). "When Jesus heard this, he withdrew from there in a boat to a desolate place" (v. 13). He wanted to regroup with His disciples and to prepare them for what lay ahead, in the not-too-distant future, for Him and for them. Since it had become impossible to get needed time alone while He was in the region of Capernaum, He decided to withdraw for a time. As Mark tells us, "He said to them, 'Come away by yourselves to a desolate place and rest a while.' For many were coming and going, and they had no leisure even to eat. And they went away in the boat to a desolate place by themselves" (Mark 6:31–32).

It is at this point that we pick up the story as John relates it. Having arrived at the lakeshore, Jesus led His men to a place in the hills, near the town of Bethsaida, the hometown of at least three of the disciples—Peter, Andrew, and Philip (John 1:44). The area He chose was somewhat remote, but since it was spring, there was "much grass in the place" (John 6:10). Also, because it was spring, "the Passover, the feast of the Jews, was at hand" (6:4). Passover was one of the most significant events of the year for the Jewish people—a celebration of God's miraculous deliverance of the Israelite people from slavery in Egypt, the exodus. The Lord's normal policy was to go to Jerusalem at Passover; this time He chose to remain in Galilee.

The time frame is important. First, Passover was a season of heightened spiritual interest. People who couldn't go to Jerusalem for whatever reason would be especially aware of their spiritual heritage during this season. God had set their ancestors free to be His people and provided for their needs by sending manna in the wilderness. Second, it was also a time when intense feelings of nationalism would be in the air. The exodus was about liberation from bondage. Galilee was a region known for strong nationalistic feelings, and the domination of the Romans made many feel that they were now enduring the bondage of another pharaoh, this time a Roman one. There was a deep longing for the coming of the promised Messiah who would free them from such oppression. For the Lord Jesus, there would also be the knowledge that, in exactly one year, He would be in Jerusalem, becoming the ultimate Passover lamb, taking on himself the sins of the world (John 1:29) by His death on the cross.

Called to Do the Impossible: Jesus's Challenge to His Disciples

> Lifting up his eyes, then, and seeing that a large crowd was coming toward him, Jesus said to Philip, "Where are we to buy bread, so that these people may eat?" He said this to test him, for he himself knew what he would do. Philip answered him, "Two hundred denarii worth of bread would not be enough for each of them to get a little." One of his

disciples, Andrew, Simon Peter's brother, said to him, "There is a boy here who has five barley loaves and two fish, but what are they for so many?" (John 6:5–9)

Jesus may have wanted to get away by himself, but the crowds had no interest in letting that happen. Bethsaida was about five to eight miles from Capernaum, along the north shore of Lake Galilee. Sensing their probable destination, crowds began spontaneously to form a massive parade, walking along the lakeshore. It swept up more and more people as it went, finally numbering in the thousands—men, women and children, sick and well. In fact, the number of men alone was five thousand, and with women, and children, it could have reached ten thousand or more. This was a remarkably high proportion of the population of the entire area! They were irresistibly drawn to Jesus—His teaching and especially His miracles—like flies to honey. Some wanted to hear Him; others to share in the spectacle; still others were desperate for healing from Him. It was truly a mass movement.

Any hope of a private retreat with His disciples vanished. When it was that Jesus lifted up his eyes and saw a large crowd, we are not told. But we are told that He reacted with characteristic compassion, not annoyance. Annoyance would have been perfectly understandable. After all, who wants someone to intrude on a much-needed vacation? I love Mark's observation: "He saw a great crowd, and he had compassion on them, because they were like sheep without a shepherd" (Mark 6:34). He had a legitimate need for time away from people, but He always chose to see people as an opportunity, not an intrusion. They had needs only He could meet, and truth only He could teach. This was an important message for His disciples (and us): *Keep an open heart to hurting people.*

Before any of the disciples could even process what their eyes were seeing, the Lord raised an issue that had not even occurred to them—what would these people eat? Now we need to recognize this was not a life-and-death issue. The crowds might have gotten hungry, but they were not in danger of starving. Their hunger might have become uncomfortable; it wasn't going to be dangerous. I suspect that none of the disciples felt responsible for feeding this mob of people. After all, these were intruders on their private time with Jesus. But people matter. They mattered to Jesus, and they must matter to those who claim to be His followers. Indifference is not an option. Self-protection cannot be our priority. That is a hard perspective to maintain in a world so full of needs, and in a culture so obsessed with rights and self.

The Lord had two seemingly opposing things He wanted to teach His disciples: their responsibility and their inadequacy. So He turned to Philip with the question: "Where are we to buy bread, so that these people may eat?" (John 6:5). John makes it very clear that the Lord wasn't really seeking information from Philip. He was in complete control of the situation, already knowing what He was going to do. The question was intended to train the disciples, not solve the problem. It was part of their preparation for the mission He would later send them on. If they needed to know their inadequacy, they had an even greater need to know His complete sufficiency.

We are not told why the Lord turned to Philip with this question. He was, as we've observed, a local boy, a native of the nearby town of Bethsaida. He could be expected to know the local resources. Perhaps that is why the Lord designated him as the point person on the food committee. Instantly, Philip found himself doing a quick mental calculation and answering a question he hadn't been asked. Jesus had asked "Where?"; Philip answered "How much?" He was a realist. What is the use of knowing where to get food if you don't have the resources to pay for it? For him, the problem wasn't one of supply but of economics: "Two hundred denarii worth of bread would not be enough" (v. 7). Since a denarius was the amount a worker would be paid for a day's labor, Philip was telling the Lord that it would require an impossible amount of money—two-thirds of a year's wages. The rest goes unsaid: "Lord, you know that we don't have that kind of cash!" Seen in purely financial terms, the problem was beyond their solution. But Philip had missed the point. He had calculated without reference to Jesus. His equation had failed to factor in the difference Jesus always makes. He was certainly not the last to make that mistake!

When Jesus had asked Philip His question, He had also spoken to the entire group of disciples: "You give them something to eat" (Mark 6:37). Apparently, in response to that command, Andrew, also a local, had set out to scour the crowd to discover what hidden resources might be available. He hadn't found very much, but what he had found he brought with him—a boy with a lunch about the size of a Happy Meal—five loaves and two small fish. His response echoed Philip's: "What are they for so many?" (John 6:9). The need was huge; the available resources were meager.

Philip and Andrew had come to the same conclusion from opposite directions. For Philip, the need was too great. For Andrew, the resources were too few. One Happy Meal and thousands of people—what good was that? And, like Philip, Andrew had left out the essential factor in the equation: the Lord Jesus. Despite all that they had experienced of Him, they still had not grasped His supernatural sufficiency.

Multiplying the Food: Experiencing the Sufficiency of Christ

Jesus said, "Have the people sit down." Now there was much grass in the place. So the men sat down, about five thousand in number. Jesus then took the loaves, and when he had given thanks, he distributed them to those who were seated. So also the fish, as much as they wanted. And when they had eaten their fill, he told his disciples, "Gather up the leftover fragments, that nothing may be lost." So they gathered them up and filled twelve baskets with fragments from the five barley loaves left by those who had eaten. When the people saw the sign that he had done, they said, "This is indeed the Prophet who is to come into the world!"

Perceiving then that they were about to come and take him by force to make him king, Jesus withdrew again to the mountain by himself. (John 6:10–15)

The Lord Jesus had not been a passive observer as all this was going on. Luke tells us that He had been both speaking to the crowds about the kingdom of God and also curing those in need of healing (Luke 9:11). As the day was ending, He switched His attention and began to give instructions to the disciples. He obviously intended to feed the crowds; perhaps more importantly, He was going to etch some indelible lessons on His disciples' minds. In doing this miracle, He would work through them in an unprecedented way, putting them at the center of action.

His first instruction was for them to seat the crowds in orderly groups of about fifty people. Anyone who has experience working with large crowds will recognize that this, in itself, was no simple task. There were good administrative reasons for seating the crowds—chiefly, to prevent a mob rush for the food—and the abundance of spring grass made it feasible. It was also a test of faith for the disciples. I can imagine the sharp comments of many as the disciples instructed them to sit down. Why? If it was to prepare for a meal, where were the catering trucks? But they persisted in their assignment, managing to get this immense throng into some semblance of order.

Jesus stilled the crowd with a brief command. Then, with every eye fixed on Him, He lifted high the boy's Happy Meal. What He was about to do had nothing to do with the crowd's faith in Him. Even His disciples were probably bewildered. Looking up to heaven, He loudly praised His Father, the God who is the source of all things. Perhaps He used words similar to a blessing still used by Jewish people: "Blessed are You, LORD our God, King of the universe, who brings forth bread from the earth." Summoning His disciples to Him, as the crowds watched in growing amazement, "He distributed [the loaves] to those who were seated. So also the fish, as much as they wanted" (John 6:11). The other gospel writers tell us that He did this through the hands of the disciples: "He broke the loaves and gave them to the disciples to set before the crowd. And they all ate and were satisfied" (Luke 9:16–17). The bread and fish were multiplied in His hands and then, like a continuous stream, filled the waiting hands of His disciples, who in turn passed them out to the crowds.

Modern skeptics offer their insights into what "really happened." Some claim that this was like a modern church sacrament, where each person takes a tiny fragment. Of course, this must ignore the plain statement of the text that all ate and were satisfied. Furthermore, five small rolls, even if they had been broken and consumed one tiny fragment at a time, wouldn't have lasted very long, and any communion-like ritual would have been unknown to people at the time. Others suggest that Jesus was engaged in a public act of shaming, aimed at those who had carefully kept their food supplies hidden. Jesus, we are told, embarrassed such selfish people into a spontaneous outpouring of generosity. There is, of course, nothing in the text to sustain such a creative reimagining of events. Besides, if Andrew had only been able to unearth one boy's small lunch, who exactly were these mysterious people carrying such immense hidden supplies of food during a spontaneous gathering of people? They are figments of skeptical imaginations.

When Jesus multiplied the food in His hands and transmitted it to the crowds through the hands of His disciples, He was not only meeting needs; He was acting out a parable for His disciples to ponder in later times. They weren't the source of the resources they carried, but simply the channels. The resources were not in them, but in their Lord. It doesn't take enormous skill to be a waiter, but you do have to know where to go to get the food! It doesn't require great ability or training to hand out what He gives us, but we do need to be smart enough to keep going back to Him. On the other hand, we must not be swamps, keeping what flows into us for ourselves, but conduits, through whom our Lord meets the needs of others.

The disciples were not just conduits; they were also recipients. The Lord had provided more than they needed (John 6:11–12). No one went hungry. Just as the Lord had fed Israel in the wilderness with bread from heaven known as manna, Jesus fed the crowds with bread in a desolate place. That image will run through the rest of John 6—Jesus is both the bread-giver and the Bread of Life. But He had not forgotten His men. Having met the needs of the crowds, He commanded them to pick up the fragments "that nothing may be lost" (v. 12). And when they obeyed Him, they discovered something amazing: that little Happy Meal not only fed thousands but twelve hampers full of bread remained. On one level, it was a common custom in a poor country to make sure that nothing was wasted. Food was precious. But this was more than frugality. They had begun the affair with a profound recognition of shortages— they didn't have either enough money or enough food. Now their "problem" was that they had more than enough.

It was obviously not coincidental that twelve disciples found themselves with twelve baskets of food, one for each disciple. Just as God had provided daily manna for the twelve tribes in the wilderness of Sinai, the Lord Jesus had provided food for each of His followers. This was another evidence of both His glorious power and His faithfulness to His obedient people. Having carried out His will by serving others, He richly provided for their needs. Having done what He told them to do, they ended up with far more than they began with.

The response of the crowds to what they had seen was both intense and misguided. Rather than being driven to listen more carefully to what Jesus had been teaching them about the kingdom of God, they determined to use Him to pursue the kingdom as they desired it to be. In His provision of food, there was an echo of Moses in the exodus (Exodus 16), and perhaps of the prophet Elisha (2 Kings 4:42–45). They knew the kind of king they wanted—a king who would defeat the Romans and elevate Israel once again to its days of former glory. But in seeing Him as "the Prophet who is to come" (John 6:14; compare Deuteronomy 18:15–22), they underestimated His true identity. In rallying "to make him king" (John 6:15), they were subverting His true authority, as if He had come to fulfill their agenda, rather than His own. They wanted a king who would serve them, not a King they would lovingly serve. But He would not be the puppet of their political and material desires. He is the sovereign Lord, and His mission was far more profound than anything they could have imagined.

Much of the Lord's intention through this miracle is revealed in the rest of John 6. In fact, the day's events would become even more remarkable for the disciples when, on their return boat trip to Capernaum, Jesus came to them at night, walking on the water (John 6:16–21). Then, He would further reveal His true identity by describing himself as the bread of life (John 6:33–35, 48, 51). The miracles and claims combine to make it clear that *the Lord Jesus was more than a prophet or a man-made king. He is the God-sent Savior,* who not only has compassion for His sheep but will lay down His life for them (John 10:11). He is the Sovereign who must be obeyed, not manipulated.

The miracle also reminds us *the Lord Jesus is the all-sufficient One,* more than enough to overcome His people's inadequacies. Although He had not needed the boy's lunch as a starter for a miracle, and although He didn't need the disciples to be distributors of the food, He had chosen to use them both. The main inadequacy the disciples displayed wasn't the inadequacy of their finances or their food resources, but the inadequacy of their faith in Him. As long as they calculated without Christ, they were helpless in the face of overwhelming needs. But when they simply obeyed Him, His sufficiency proved to be more than enough to meet not only the needs of the crowds but their own needs as well.

But there is another message in the failure of the crowds. They experienced one of the most remarkable events in human history, but they had completely missed the message. *The Lord Jesus warns that we can miss the significant in the midst of the sensational.* The impact of the miracle had stopped at their stomachs. They wanted a king who would meet their needs and satisfy their physical desires. They had gladly received His gifts, but they had missed His true message. As He would tell them the next day: "Truly, truly, I say to you, you are seeking me, not because you saw signs, but because you ate your fill of the loaves. Do not work for the food that perishes, but for the food that endures to eternal life, which the Son of Man will give to you. For on him God the Father has set his seal" (John 6:26–27). That is a warning we must be sure to hear.

ELEVEN

MASTER OF SURPRISE

As a young man, the British poet W. H. Auden turned his back on his family's Christian heritage and became an ardent atheist. But in 1940, at the age of thirty-three, he declared himself a believer in Christ. A few years later he described the reason he came to faith in Jesus in a rather surprising way: "I believe because He fulfills none of my dreams, because He is in every respect the opposite of what He would be if I could have made him in my own image."[1]

I'm not sure I could or would say it like that, but the truth remains that the entire life of our Lord Jesus is one of continual surprises. We know the story, so it is hard for us to see how consistently the Lord took people by surprise, even those who were the most committed to Him. He didn't conform to the expectations of His contemporaries, nor will He conform to ours, no matter how hard we try to domesticate Him. The "gentle Jesus, meek and mild" of our Sunday school days just isn't the Jesus we meet in the Gospels.

Jesus may not always have been predictable, but He was always reliable. He may not have done what others expected in the way they expected, but everything He did was fully consistent with who He was and is—the Son of God. There is probably no place in the Gospels where we see Jesus as the master of surprise more clearly than in the miracles we are going to consider in this chapter. But we can be sure that even when He seemed to be acting "out of character," He had good and sufficient reasons.

A Short Walk to a Distant World

> And from there he arose and went away to the region of Tyre and Sidon. And he entered a house and did not want anyone to know, yet he could not be hidden. (Mark 7:24)

Jesus's confrontation with the Jewish leaders in Jerusalem that we considered in chapter 9, as well as the profound impact made by the feeding of the five thousand in the previous chapter, meant that He was now a public figure of such importance that He could not be ignored. Mark 7 begins by telling us that the Jewish leaders had sent an investigative committee to Galilee, not so much to gather information about Him as to gather ammunition to use against Him. Back in His home area, a new controversy erupted, this time about another cherished Jewish identity—food laws and traditions. The Old Testament had established a list of prohibited foods, and to protect these, the rabbis had established a long list of kosher requirements, designed to "put a hedge around Torah."

Those traditions were perhaps well-intentioned, but like virtually all human additions to God's Word, they became ends in themselves, vested with tremendous authority and defended with great vigor. In response, Jesus made two assertions that only served to further inflame the traditionalists' animosity toward Him. First, He insisted that true "cleanness" wasn't primarily about external contamination, but something much deeper—the internal corruption of the human heart (Mark 7:14–15, 21–23). Second, and even more dramatic, He claimed that His presence meant that the time for all those food laws had ended (Mark 7:18–19). By His coming, God's new era had arrived! That, by any measure, was a stunning claim. As a result, the Jewish leaders' determination to put an end to Jesus only hardened.

It is in this context that we read a deceptively simple geographical statement: "He arose and went away to the region of Tyre and Sidon" (Mark 7:24). In terms of physical distance, this was only a matter of a few dozen miles. In terms of religious, cultural, historical, and spiritual significance, it was like jumping the Grand Canyon.

Tyre and Sidon lie to the northwest of Galilee in Phoenicia, an area that is today known as Lebanon. Tyre, about forty miles from Capernaum, was the powerhouse of the region, a major trading port with a diverse population and major influence over Galilee's economy. More importantly, Tyre along with its partner city, Sidon, was one of Israel's ancient enemies. Sidon was the home of the notorious Jezebel, the wife of Ahab and the killer of the prophets in the time of Elijah (1 Kings 16:31). Deeply pagan, the region was the target of some of the Old Testament prophets' harshest denunciations. A few years after the time of Jesus, the Jewish historian Josephus makes it clear that the animosity remained intense: "The Egyptians, the whole race without exception, and among the Phoenicians, the Tyrians, are notoriously our bitterest enemies."[2]

For these reasons, Phoenicia was a very unlikely place for the Lord Jesus to seek refuge. This was not an overnight stay; He would spend months in the region. Importantly, He had not left Galilee out of fear of the Jews. Rather, in obedience to His Father's timing, He was choosing to delay the inevitable eruption of conflict. But there was another, less obvious reason. He had taken His disciples with Him, leading them further and further out of their cultural comfort zone. This must have seemed very strange to them. After all, when He had commissioned them for their earlier mission, He had been very clear: "Go nowhere among the Gentiles and enter no town of the Samaritans, but go rather to the lost sheep of the house of Israel" (Matthew 10:5–6). Now He was leading them into the very places He had commanded them not to go! What was this all about?

Although He does not explicitly say so, it seems clear that one of His primary reasons for this move into Gentile territory was to prepare His men for the mission into which He would launch them after His resurrection. These were the men the risen Lord would command, "Go . . . and make disciples of all nations" (Matthew 28:19) and to bear witness to Him "to the end of the earth" (Acts 1:8). Many of them would spend much of the rest of their lives well outside their Jewish comfort zone, beyond the borders of the Promised Land. As part of their training, He was leading them into Gentile territory. Even more radically, He entered a home to stay there; it was quite possibly a Gentile home. This was a radical break from their past, but if they were going to carry out the mission He had for them, they needed to see people in an entirely different way. The principle applies to us as well: *We can't become the people God calls us to be until we begin to see the world and its people as He does.*

Strange Encounter: Jesus and a Desperate Gentile Mother

But immediately a woman whose little daughter had an unclean spirit heard of him and came and fell down at his feet. Now the woman was a Gentile, a Syrophoenician by birth. And she begged him to cast the demon out of her daughter. And he said to her, "Let the children be fed first, for it is not right to take the children's bread and throw it to the dogs." But she answered him, "Yes, Lord; yet even the dogs under the table eat the children's crumbs." And he said to her, "For this statement you may go your way; the demon has left your daughter." And she went home and found the child lying in bed and the demon gone. (Mark 7:25–30)

Jesus, Mark has said, did not want anyone to know of His presence. But it was not to be. No matter how discreet Jesus was, His presence quickly became known, even here in foreign territory. His reputation had already spread far and wide, as we were told in Mark 3:7–8: "Jesus withdrew with his disciples to the sea, and a great crowd followed, from Galilee and Judea and Jerusalem and Idumea and from beyond the Jordan and *from around Tyre and Sidon.* When the great crowd heard all that he was doing, they came to him" (emphasis added). So when word that the Jewish healer and wonder-worker was there reached the crowds at the local wells, the news spread rapidly.

Desperation acknowledges no political boundaries and disregards normal manners. Jesus may have wanted privacy, but it was not to be. For one distressed mother, His presence brought a ray of hope into a very dark home. We are not told how she had come to know about Jesus, but she clearly had, and she believed that if anyone could help her suffering daughter, He could. So, with the determination unique to a loving and distraught mother, she set out to enlist the Healer's help.

She knew enough about Jewish men to know that she had no standing or credentials to gain access to a Jewish rabbi. She was ceremonially unclean and a foreigner to Him. She would, she knew, be seen as a pagan from the land of Jezebel, the home of Baal worship. And she was a woman, living in a world dominated by men determined to keep women in their place. But none of those things could deter her. She was a mother on a mission for her helpless child.

At this point it is helpful to turn to the account in Matthew's gospel, which describes what transpired in more detail:

And behold, a Canaanite woman from that region came out and was crying, "Have mercy on me, O Lord, Son of David; my daughter is severely oppressed by a demon." But he did not answer her a word. And his disciples came and begged him, saying, "Send her away, for she is crying out after us." He answered, "I was sent only to the lost sheep of the house of Israel." But she came and knelt before him, saying, "Lord, help me." And he answered, "It is not right to take the children's bread and throw it to the dogs." She said, "Yes, Lord, yet even the dogs eat the crumbs that fall from their masters' table." Then Jesus answered her, "O woman, great is your faith! Be it done for you as you desire." And her daughter was healed instantly. (Matthew 15:22–28)

Apparently she knew exactly where to find Jesus, presumably at the house where He was residing. She made no attempt to be subtle about her reasons for coming. As Matthew tells us, she kept on crying out, "Have mercy on me, O Lord, Son of David; my daughter is severely oppressed by a demon" (Matthew 15:22). She addressed Jesus in a remarkable way: "Son of David" was a title for the Jewish Messiah. This is strongly Jewish language. How much did she really know about Jesus? Did she really believe what she was saying? And her appeal was for mercy. She made no claim but that of her daughter's misery. And she had no intention of going away quietly. She kept crying out after Him. If she had to be a public nuisance, she would gladly pay that price.

At this point the story takes a completely unexpected turn. From what we know of Jesus, we expect Him to turn toward her in compassion, to calm the distraught mother with gentle words, and to heal her daughter. But that's not what happened. Instead, we have an encounter unlike any other in the Gospels. Jesus seems to act in a manner that is entirely out of character, in a way incompatible with all that we otherwise know about Him. But before we jump to any hasty conclusions, we need to exercise caution. When someone you know well and trust completely seems to act "out of character," it is wise to suspend judgment, to give that person the benefit of the doubt. He may have reasons that are not yet clear to you.

Jesus met her anguished cries with a strange silence: "He did not answer her a word" (v. 23). Nowhere else has Jesus ignored someone who came for help, and we have already seen His special sensitivity to parents with sick or dying children. He has also consistently shown mercy and compassion for Gentiles—the demonized man, the centurion with the dying daughter, the Samaritan woman at the well, recorded in John 4. But His silence here didn't silence the woman. She persisted in her appeals, until the disciples came to the Lord, begging Him to stop her, perhaps because of all the unwanted attention her behavior was attracting: "Send her away, for she is crying out after us" (v. 23). My guess is that they were saying, "She's a nuisance. Please, just do what she's asking, and we'll be rid of her."

The Lord once again catches us off guard. In response to the disciples' request, He said, not only to His disciples but also to the woman, "I was sent only to the lost sheep of the house of Israel" (v. 24). How was this an answer to their demand? It seems that He was only confirming their request to send her away. But He was doing much more. He was declaring that the Father's mission for Him was in direct fulfillment of the promises and prophecies of the Old Testament, that salvation would come to the nations by coming first to and through the nation of Israel. As we have seen, this was the mission He had given to His own disciples in Matthew 10:5–6.

He had also made clear to the Samaritan woman, "Salvation is from the Jews" (John 4:22). God's purposes in history gave priority and prominence to Israel. To them and through them the gospel was going to come to the world. But, as the outcome of His death and resurrection would reveal, the Lord's mission to Israel would lead to the cross, and through His death and resurrection, salvation would be made possible for those of every nation who put their faith and trust in Him.

Whatever the woman made of the Lord's words, she pressed on, approaching as closely as she could to Jesus, kneeling before Him, and renewing her heartrending plea: "Lord, help me" (Matthew 15:25). And once again Jesus's reply befuddles us: "It is not right to take the children's bread and throw it to the dogs" (v. 26).

There is perhaps nothing the Lord ever did or said that has incited more "righteous indignation" than this. On its face, the words are jarring, and some have accused the Lord of overt racism. There is no doubt that "children" refers to the Jews, the descendants of Abraham to whom God had made covenant promises. Israel could make a claim on Messiah that no other people could, on the basis of God's covenant promises. This Gentile woman had no such claim, and she knew it. She was an outsider to the "family," in that sense. That means that "dogs" describes non-Jews. What we cannot see from our English translations is that the Lord has chosen His word for "dog" carefully. He did not use the term that normally describes the scavenger dogs that were the bane of the ancient world. Those untamed dogs were wild and often dangerous, roaming the streets in packs. Rather, He chose a word often used of a family pet that lived in the family compound. They were not "family," but neither were they total outsiders.

The words sound harsher than they, in fact, were. As Mark Strauss observes, "Jesus is intentionally provoking her faith. . . . He wants to see the woman claim what is rightfully hers, which is access to God's salvation, but He does so provocatively."[3] Jesus was using a kind of mini-parable, and the woman seemed to realize that. She was not insulted by the Lord's words. In fact, she had been listening carefully enough to hear the Lord's "loophole." He had not shut the door on feeding the dogs, but simply said the children have priority. They get fed first. But what about "leftovers"?

The woman seized her opening. She was more than willing to admit that she had no "family rights," no privileged place at the family table, as the Jewish people had. She was willing to admit that she wasn't one of the children of Abraham, and she wasn't asking to jump the queue, to take what rightfully belonged to others. She wasn't claiming her rights; she was declaring her need. And she would take whatever the Lord was willing to give, because she was completely convinced that He could give her what she needed, without in any way robbing the "children" of their rights. The Lord's power was so great that He was fully able to meet her needs with "leftovers."

Her response obviously delighted the Lord: "O woman, great is your faith! Be it done for you as you desire" (v. 28). Her knowledge of Jesus and of theological truth was obviously meager. But her faith and trust in Jesus and His power, as well as her confidence in His grace and kindness, were profound. It is striking that Jesus commends two people in the Gospels for their faith: this woman and the centurion (Matthew 8:10), both of them Gentiles. In the light of that faith, Mark tells us that Jesus then said, "For this statement you may go your way; the demon has left your daughter" (Mark 7:29). The woman's faith in the Lord's word was almost as remarkable as her faith in His power. With nothing to go on except His word, she anxiously rushed home to her daughter, happy to discover that she had received the miracle she had so ardently pursued. And the disciples had once again seen vivid evidence that the Lord's power and compassion were not circumscribed by the boundaries of the Promised Land.

Jesus Meets the Needs of a Disabled Pagan Man

> Then he returned from the region of Tyre and went through Sidon to the Sea of Galilee, in the region of the Decapolis. And they brought to him a man who was deaf and had a speech impediment, and they begged him to lay his hand on him. And taking him aside from the crowd privately, he put his fingers into his ears, and after spitting touched his tongue. And looking up to heaven, he sighed and said to him, "Ephphatha," that is, "Be opened." And his ears were opened, his tongue was released, and he spoke plainly. And Jesus charged them to tell no one. But the more he charged them, the more zealously they proclaimed it. And they were astonished beyond measure, saying, "He has done all things well. He even makes the deaf hear and the mute speak." (Mark 7:31–37)

Because most of us are not familiar with the geography of the Holy Land, the travel itinerary that begins this section will not immediately strike us as unusual. But saying that He returned from Tyre to Galilee by way of Sidon and the Decapolis is something like saying that Jesus returned from San Diego to Los Angeles by way of Phoenix and Las Vegas. Sidon was about twenty-five miles north of Tyre, away from Galilee, not toward it. Going from Sidon through the Decapolis to Galilee would mean a circle route through modern Lebanon, and around the east side of Lake Galilee into the Gentile area of the Decapolis and finally back home to Capernaum and Galilee. A direct line back through Galilee to the Decapolis would have been far shorter and quicker. The route He followed, on the other hand, would take weeks, and would keep them in Gentile territory the entire time. In other words, this journey would be an extended exposure to Gentile peoples and culture, the kinds of places where some of them would later travel as His ambassadors.

For the time being, the final destination on this circuitous journey was the Decapolis, a league of ten cities, most of them in modern Jordan. They were Greco-Roman in origin and culture, and had banded together for mutual defense. Jesus and the disciples had, in fact, traveled down to the southeast corner of Lake Galilee, to an area with a heavily Gentile population. Here, in this most unexpected place, people again responded to the presence of Jesus, recognizing His power. It is entirely possible that Jesus's reputation had spread to this location because of the testimony of the man who had been delivered of the legion of demons. As you might remember, that man had begged for the privilege of joining Jesus and His disciples, but the Lord had refused. Instead, He commissioned him, "Go home to your friends and tell them how much the Lord has done for you, and how he has had mercy on you" (Mark 5:19). Obediently, the man complied. "He went away and began to proclaim in the Decapolis how much Jesus had done for him, and everyone marveled" (Mark 5:20). Now that same Jesus was here in their midst!

An unidentified group of people knew enough about Jesus to believe that He could help a man who was unable to hear or to speak in an intelligible way, a condition that shut him off from any normal means of communication with others. We have no way of knowing how he came to this state. Was he born this way? Was it the result of a disease or an accident? We don't, and can't, know. But he had friends who cared enough to bring him to Jesus in the hope that he would be healed. Once again, Gentiles were showing faith in Jesus that was so often missing among His own people!

Perhaps to avoid making a spectacle of the man, Jesus chose to take him away from the crowd so that He could deal with him privately and personally. The Lord never treated hurting people as props or side-show spectacles to enhance His fame. He never exploited sufferers to elevate himself or to amuse or astonish an audience. He treated each sufferer with grace and dignity. Once again, His method was unique, using physical touch on the affected organs, personalizing His healing in a way entirely appropriate for a man unable either to hear or to speak. First, He placed His fingers in the man's ears. Then, apparently spitting on His hand, He placed His finger on the man's tongue, the saliva from His mouth mixing with the man's own. Then, looking to heaven and sighing or groaning, He spoke a single word of command in Aramaic to a man unable to hear it: "Ephphatha" ("Be opened"). The result was instantaneous: a deaf, mute man heard and spoke clearly. In an instant, at Jesus's touch and word, the impossible had become actual!

Once again, Jesus instructed the man and those who had brought him to Jesus ("them") not to talk of this to others. And just as before, this hardly seems feasible, but it underlines Jesus's intention not to be known as a mere miracle-worker. But loosened tongues won't be stilled, and so as the group dispersed, they began celebrating the works of Jesus to all who would listen. It is one of the great declarations of the Gospels, found on the lips of Gentiles, "He has done all things well. He even makes the deaf hear and the mute speak" (Mark 7:37).

These people had no way of knowing that their words were echoing the words of the prophet Isaiah, spoken more than seven hundred years earlier. They probably had never even heard of Isaiah, and had certainly never read Isaiah 35. There the prophet celebrates the blessing King Messiah would bring:

> Then the eyes of the blind shall be opened,
> and the ears of the deaf unstopped;
> then shall the lame man leap like a deer,
> and the tongue of the mute sing for joy.
> For waters break forth in the wilderness,
> and streams in the desert. . . .
> And the ransomed of the LORD shall return

and come to Zion with singing;
everlasting joy shall be upon their heads;
they shall obtain gladness and joy,
and sorrow and sighing shall flee away.

(Isaiah 35:5–6, 10)

Ironically, Gentiles celebrate that Messiah was in their midst using biblical terms. All the while, supposed scriptural experts had failed to acknowledge the fulfillment of God's Word in the person and deeds of Jesus. So it is Gentiles who were entering into the messianic blessings through Jesus, without having had to become Jews, while Jewish leaders clung to their spiritual blindness.

This excursion outside of the land of Israel with Jesus had been full of significance for the disciples, as it should be for us. It showed that the basis of experiencing Messiah's power was faith, not ethnicity. Believing Gentiles had received the blessings of Messiah, not by becoming Jews, but by trusting the Lord Jesus. It also laid the foundation for their later understanding, that although Jesus had *come to* the Jewish people in fulfillment of God's ancient promises, He had also *come for* believing Gentiles. As Paul will later write, the gospel is "the power of God for salvation to everyone who believes, to the Jew first and also to the Greek" (Romans 1:16). But Jews who do not believe in the Lord Jesus will be shut out from the blessings of that gospel.

For the disciples, this uncomfortable venture into Gentile territory had been the training ground for the task of bringing the good news of the Savior to people of every tribe and tongue and nation. For those of us who have entered into the promises of Messiah through faith in Him, He truly has done "all things well." But our enjoyment of our blessings must drive us to look across the borders of our divided world with a vision to take the gospel message to those yet to hear, know, and worship Him.

TWELVE

—∿∿—

BUT NOW I SEE

Manoj Yadav was born in a remote village in northern India, far from expert medical care. Although his parents didn't recognize it until he began to bump into things when crawling, Manoj had been born congenitally blind by cataracts. Over the years, doctors in the region told the family that their son would never see. But when he was eighteen, some eye specialists visited his village and stirred up hope that an operation might give him sight. He and his father traveled thirteen hours by train to India's capital, where, at a charity eye hospital, skilled surgeons replaced his cataract-covered lenses with synthetic ones.

A day later, they removed his bandages. His world was suddenly filled with light, but his brain couldn't unscramble the onslaught of visual images it was suddenly receiving. He couldn't distinguish people from objects, or where one thing ended and another began. However, over the next months, his brain began to make sense of the signals it was receiving. "It took me about one and a half years before I could see anything clearly. . . . Now I can even ride a bicycle through a crowded market."[1]

Few things are more precious to us than our sight, especially if something happens to threaten or damage our eyes. I have a good friend who became blind from an infection just after birth, and I am always amazed at his zest for life and his ability to function so well in a world he has never seen. I had the privilege of officiating at his wedding, and as his beautifully presented bride began to make her way down the aisle, I almost began to cry with sadness, knowing that he couldn't physically delight in this vision of her beauty. "Fred, she looks lovely!" I said, and then tried to find a few words to describe her. I can only imagine what he felt at that moment.

As a college student, I found myself in a battle for my own eyesight when I suffered a retinal detachment. For years since, I've been grateful that modern medicine returned most of my sight in that eye to me. But then, recently, my wife suffered a traumatic eye injury while she was pruning a tree so that we could get a better look at our bird feeder from the house. During her pruning, a large branch sprang back and hit her. The damage was catastrophic, puncturing her eyeball, impacting almost everything, and causing massive damage to her entire eye. After a very long operation, the doctor described the surgery as possibly the most difficult he had ever had to perform. He declared, somewhat hopefully, "I think I've saved your eye, but I don't know if I've saved your sight." He had, but only in a very partial way. Multiple doctors' visits and treatments over the following months have resulted in the restoration of some vision, but both Elizabeth and I are constantly reminded of how precious the gift of sight is.

I don't know if you've ever noticed, but with all the remarkable miracles in the Old Testament, none of them involve the restoration of sight to a blind person. As well, the book of Acts records many miracles done through the apostles, but again, none of them gave sight to the blind. (There is, of course, the account of Ananias restoring Saul's sight in Acts 9, but Saul's condition was not a natural ailment, but rather the result of his encounter with the risen Lord on the road to Damascus.) All this makes it even more striking when we turn to the Gospels and encounter five distinct episodes in which the Lord Jesus heals seven blind people. We are also told that He healed other blind people, mentioned in passages summarizing Jesus's healing ministry.[2]

The Lord's miracles were obviously acts of power, as we have seen. But, more than that, they were signs that accredit His claims, reveal His character, and point to His provision of salvation, all with the purpose of drawing people to faith in Him. The story we are given in John 9 is one of the most compelling in the entire Bible, not simply because of the remarkable miracle, but because of the reaction it arouses and the dialogue that results. The encounter reveals there is a blindness far more common and far more disastrous than physical blindness: spiritual blindness. And if spiritual blindness is a worse problem than physical blindness, then spiritual sight is an even greater gift than physical sight is.

As we have been tracking the ministry of the Lord Jesus, we now find ourselves once again in Jerusalem, at the time of the Feast of Booths (John 7:2). This feast, also known as *Sukkoth* or the Feast of Tabernacles, occurs in the holiest month of the year, in the late summer or early fall, on the heels of the Day of Atonement. We are now only about six months from the Lord's final Passover, and the clock is ticking toward the judicial murder of the Lord Jesus, the central purpose of His life and ministry.

Living in the Darkness: The Plight of a Man Born Blind

> As he passed by, he saw a man blind from birth. And his disciples asked him, "Rabbi, who sinned, this man or his parents, that he was born blind?" Jesus answered, "It was not that this man sinned, or his parents, but that the works

of God might be displayed in him. We must work the works of him who sent me while it is day; night is coming, when no one can work. As long as I am in the world, I am the light of the world." (John 9:1–5)

As we observe this story, we need to read it against the backdrop of the growing tension between the Lord Jesus and the Jewish leadership. The religious establishment has opposed Jesus throughout His entire ministry, and now, during this festival season in Jerusalem, there is a new level of intensity. Temperatures began to rise during the Feast of Tabernacles itself, when Jesus loudly proclaimed in the temple courtyards, "If anyone thirsts, let him come to me and drink. Whoever believes in me, as the Scripture has said, 'Out of his heart will flow rivers of living water'" (John 7:37–38). When many responded positively, it aroused debate about Jesus in the general population, which in turn made the Jewish leaders all the more determined to put a stop to Him. But Jesus would not be stopped. Shortly after the festival itself, He made another declaration that incited even deeper conflict: "I am the light of the world. Whoever follows me will not walk in darkness, but will have the light of life" (John 8:12). That astonishing claim fueled a debate that grew in intensity until Jesus's most startling claim: "Truly, truly, I say to you, before Abraham was, I am" (John 8:58). The Jewish leaders recognized the significance: He was claiming for himself the very name God had used to describe himself: "I AM" (Exodus 3:14). That claim rang in their ears as an unimaginable blasphemy, "so they picked up stones to throw at him, but Jesus hid himself and went out of the temple" (John 8:59). The situation had turned murderous.

When tempers had somewhat cooled, Jesus and His disciples returned to the temple courtyards. Beggars are not uncommon in religious places even now, since the presence of religiously minded crowds brings the hope that some will exercise charity. But beggars also can simply become part of the furniture at such places, hardly noticed or deliberately ignored by the gathering crowds. Still, amid the throngs of people, Jesus noticed a blind beggar, a man "blind from birth" (9:1). Just as He had seen the lame man among the crowds by the pool, so now He saw this man, and drew the disciples' attention to him.

Blindness was tragically common in the ancient world, often due to water-born postnatal infections or congenital cataracts. In many parts of the modern world, it remains a persistent problem. This man, however, was blind from birth. How the disciples knew that isn't immediately clear. But what is clear is that this wasn't a temporary, psychological, or treatable problem. This man had never seen. As a result, he was a beggar, trying to provide for himself in virtually the only way a blind person could. Even today, the presence of blind or disabled beggars in the developing world or, sadly, among the homeless in prosperous Western countries is heartbreaking.

Perhaps because Jesus had drawn their attention to him, the disciples asked the Lord a question, maybe one that had long been gnawing at the back of their minds as they dealt with so many desperately needy people: "Rabbi, who sinned, this man or his parents, that he was born blind?" (v. 2). The assumption is clear: all such suffering was due to personal sin. So there must be a direct causal link between each case of suffering and a person's sin. They were not alone. This was a common idea in the ancient world. It is, sadly, an assumption that even some Christians make today when they declare to another, "You could be healed, if you'd just confess your sin!" It is, of course, an assumption that ignores the entire message of the book of Job.

The disciples were wise enough to bring their question to Jesus, but we shouldn't ignore their insensitivity. After all, the man was blind, not deaf, as they stood talking about him. We can too easily treat disabled people as if they aren't fully human. In the disciples' minds, there were only two options: either his parents sinned and he's paying their penalty, or somehow he had sinned in the womb. (Some rabbis claimed that an unborn baby could sin, a view that, while somewhat bizarre, does endow the unborn with personhood, in contrast to too many modern views.)

Jesus's direct rebuttal is important: "It was not that this man sinned, or his parents, but that the works of God might be displayed in him" (v. 3). Suffering is a reality in our groaning world, and individual cases cannot be simplistically blamed on an act of sin or a lack of faith. *Not all suffering is directly due to sin.* Obviously, some suffering is directly connected to our sin or stupidity. The Lord doesn't deny that. And all suffering is, in the final analysis, due to the entrance of sin into God's good creation, so that we live in a fallen world. But a great deal of suffering, including this man's, is not causally linked to a person's sin. There is a profound mystery about suffering, and simplistic answers dishonor God. At the same time, *although suffering is mysterious, it is nevertheless within God's sovereign, gracious purposes.* With the simple expression "but that," the Lord declared that this man's condition was not haphazard or random. It lay within God's providential rule of the world. He is, after all, the one "who works all things according to the counsel of his will" (Ephesians 1:11), and our inability to comprehend His purpose does not mean He lacks one. Furthermore, *our suffering, like this man's, may well serve as a platform for God's glory.* Our greatest good is not our personal comfort, but God's glory. The Lord may reveal His glory by preserving us from suffering. He may do so by delivering us from suffering, as He does here. Or He may do so by sustaining us through suffering, for our good and His glory.

The Lord would not allow them to turn this man into an object of speculation. He was not an object lesson, but an image-bearer.

The Lord's disciples needed to see that he was not a theological problem to be solved, but a person to help: "We must work the works of him who sent me while it is day; night is coming, when no one can work" (John 9:4). By using "we," Jesus changed the focus. We are called not to speculate, but to serve with Him in His mission, sharing His works, recognizing the time is short. Then Jesus once again reminded them of His claim, made earlier in John 8:12: "I am the light of the world" (v. 5). Perhaps His introductory words were meant to remind them of what He had also said about His followers: "You are the light of the world" (Matthew 5:14).

Dispelling the Darkness: Physical Healing for a Blind Man

> Having said these things, he spit on the ground and made mud with the saliva. Then he anointed the man's eyes with the mud and said to him, "Go, wash in the pool of Siloam" (which means Sent). So he went and washed and came back seeing. (John 9:6–7)

What followed occurred entirely at the Lord's initiative. As far as we can tell, the blind man had been completely passive and quiet while the conversation about his condition had transpired. Jesus made no attempt to introduce himself to the man, to declare His credentials, or to seek his permission for what He was about to do. This was an act of sovereign grace, not a response to faith. We will see his faith grow as we move through the story, but there is no evidence of faith at this point. He had no suspicion that he was about to experience a miracle. As he will protest later to his interrogators, "Never since the world began has it been heard that anyone opened the eyes of a man born blind" (9:32). And yet, the promise was clear. When Messiah came, "the eyes of the blind shall see" (Isaiah 29:18; compare 35:5; 42:7).

We have seen repeatedly that the Lord's methods follow no discernable pattern. This time He began by spitting, as He had before when He healed a deaf man with a speech impediment (Mark 7:32–37), as well as a blind man (Mark 8:22–26). But this time He spat on the ground to make mud and then smeared the mud on the man's eyes. Having done that, He ordered the man to go and wash at the pool of Siloam. This combination is unique to this miracle.

The command to go to the pool of Siloam calls us to get our bearings in the city of Jerusalem. Located on a hill, Jerusalem was vulnerable to water shortages. The major source was the Gihon Spring, which was in a valley and therefore susceptible to enemy attack in times of war. Seven hundred years earlier, when Jerusalem had been threatened by a siege from the armies of Assyria, King Hezekiah had ordered a tunnel to be dug through the rock to a pool at the southern end of the walled city. It was a remarkable achievement, one that tourists today can see for themselves by ducking their way through the tunnel's nearly 600 yards. By the Lord's time, water from that spring was tunneled through underground rock-hewn channels to a pool, called Siloam (a word meaning "sent'), constructed where two valleys converge. Interestingly, that first-century pool was uncovered in 2004 by workers refurbishing a sewer line in the area. The northern end of the pool is now visible.

The pool of Siloam is about 350 feet below and a half-mile's walk from the temple mount, where Jesus encountered the blind man. In other words, His simple command to go and wash required the blind man to navigate his way through festival-crowded, winding streets with mud blobs over his eyes, on the unstated promise that, when he washed the mud off, something would happen.

There is an important fact that John hides from us until verse 14: these events were taking place on a Sabbath day. The Lord Jesus was once again directly challenging Jewish tradition about the meaning of the Sabbath by performing a miracle on the Sabbath day, just as He had done at least six times previously. At the same time, by having the miracle take place some distance from Him, He may have been seeking to prevent another major disruption in the temple courts.

What Jesus asked the man to do was far from easy. But there must have been something in the Lord's authoritative and yet compassionate tone that inspired him to do what he had been told to do. Was it the thought that he had nothing to lose by the attempt and everything to gain? Was it because the mysterious man's words stirred something deep within him to an unexplainable hope? We are not told. But Elaine Phillips perceptively suggests: "Even the journey was a walk of faith as he was a known figure in these parts and people would ask him why the curious wads of mud were on his face and where he was headed."[3]

It all ended so quickly. When he finally reached the pool, he stepped in, washed his face, and was suddenly able to open his eyes and to see! Think of it in light of the way we began this chapter. His eyes were able to see images and his brain was immediately able to make sense of what they meant. The miracle was complex— not only had his eyes been restored but his brain had been rewired to do what it had never done before. His was an instant, complex, and complete healing.

We can only imagine his emotions at that moment—disbelief, confusion, amazement, overwhelming joy! John puts it so simply: the man "came back seeing." But even better things were to come.

Entering into Light: Delivered from Spiritual Blindness

The neighbors and those who had seen him before as a beggar were saying, "Is this not the man who used to sit and beg?" Some said, "It is he." Others said, "No, but he is like him." He kept saying, "I am the man." So they said to him,

"Then how were your eyes opened?" He answered, "The man called Jesus made mud and anointed my eyes and said to me, 'Go to Siloam and wash.' So I went and washed and received my sight." They said to him, "Where is he?" He said, "I do not know."

They brought to the Pharisees the man who had formerly been blind. Now it was a Sabbath day when Jesus made the mud and opened his eyes. (John 9:8–14)

Where would you go, if something like that happened to you? Back to the place where you were known, where you had spent so many years of your life with others who had problems like yours? I'm sure there were some who celebrated the man's return with glad astonishment, when they saw their now formerly blind friend walking toward them. Their eyes were even more wide open in amazement than his! But, as John tells the story, the prevailing reaction was one of confusion and consternation. He looked completely different and yet hauntingly familiar. Was this really the same man or a relative playing a nasty trick?

But when they pressed him for answers, he left no doubt: "Of course it's me!"

"But how did it happen?"

"I can't really say. All I know is a man named Jesus put mud on my eyes, told me to go and wash in the pool of Siloam. So I did—and then I could see!"

"And where's this Jesus now?"

"I have no idea—and even if I could see Him, I wouldn't recognize Him. I've never seen His face."

The Jewish leaders were looking to catch Jesus one way or another and had put the word out on the street about Him. We will read later in the chapter that the man's parents were terrified when they were called in for questioning by the Jewish investigators:

"They feared the Jews [that is, the Jewish leaders], for the Jews had already agreed that if anyone should confess Jesus to be Christ, he was to be put out of the synagogue" (9:22). Faced with an undeniable miracle but also the fact that the notorious Jesus was somehow entangled in what had happened, the man's neighbors decided the only safe thing to do was to refer the matter to the authorities.

When the Jewish authorities heard what had happened, they quickly realized they were dealing with a significant problem. They could not deny that a once blind man could now see, try as they might. The evidence was standing directly in front of them. They wouldn't celebrate it, as they should, since that would undermine their determined rejection of Jesus, giving credibility to His remarkable claims. So they seized on legalistic nonsense: "He made mud on the Sabbath so he must be a God-forsaken sinner." They made every effort to discredit the miracle. They even attempted to intimidate the man's parents into admitting that their son wasn't born blind at all. Despite all the evidence before them, they refused to see. They would cling to the traditions and buttress their irrational rejection of Jesus, because they felt they had too much to lose by embracing reality. The feisty healed man saw through all their subterfuge with an irrefutable challenge: "One thing I do know, that though I was blind, now I see. . . . This is an amazing thing! You do not know where he comes from, and yet he opened my eyes" (John 9:25, 30).

Light not only illuminates; it also exposes and even blinds. I have had people say to me, "I would believe if I saw a miracle." But history and experience show that such a claim is almost never true. As the old adage says, "There are none so blind as those who will not see." Or, "Convince a man against his will, he's of the same opinion still." Too many practice a selective skepticism. The problem is not an insufficiency of evidence, but a refusal to bow the knee to Jesus.

Sadly we do not have the space here to pursue "the rest of the story." I would encourage you to take the time to do that. Jesus was not content to leave the man with his physical sight alone. It is interesting to see the man's growing awareness of Jesus's true identity. When questioned by the crowds, he spoke simply of "the man called Jesus" (v. 11). Confronted by the Jewish leaders, he first insisted, "He is a prophet" (v. 17). As they pressed him harder, he asserted that Jesus was "from God" (v. 33). He had come a long way, but not far enough.

After the Jewish leaders cast the healed man out of their presence, Jesus then sought out the man in the crowds. In a brief but remarkable exchange, Jesus declared himself to be "the Son of Man" (v. 35). The response was immediate: "He said, 'Lord, I believe,' and he worshiped him" (v. 38). This is a significant example of the nature of true faith. "Blind faith" is believing without evidence. True faith is grounded on good and sufficient evidence. This man could see that evidence through eyes made new by the One standing before him. And as Jesus had said, "I am the light of the world. Whoever follows me will not walk in darkness, but will have the light of life" (John 8:12). In that moment, the man born blind had been born from above and entered into eternal light. The healing of his physical blindness had been a wonderful gift; the healing of his spiritual blindness was an even greater and more lasting one.

The Lord Jesus truly is the light of the world, and of everyone who puts their faith in Him. C. S. Lewis helpfully wrote, "I believe in Christianity as I believe that the Sun has risen, not only because I see it but because by it, I see everything else."[4] Light and sight are amazing gifts. Everything changes when they are present. At the deepest level of our lives, Jesus is "the light of life" (John 8:12). And the man's response is the response of true faith: he worshipped Him. Seeing Jesus for who He is puts us on our knees before Him.

But light rejected is blindness chosen. Jesus warned of that when He told some of His most adamant critics, "If they do not hear Moses and the Prophets, neither will they be convinced if someone should rise from the dead" (Luke 16:31). And this miracle is evidence of that. People who are set in their unbelief will not believe, even when a living miracle is standing right in front of them.

Our culture presses in on us with coercive power to see what it sees, to say what it says, to live as it lives. The claims of Jesus are as directly countercultural in our world as they were in the world of first-century Jerusalem. He calls us to enter into the kingdom of light, to kneel with the once blind man before the sight-giving, life-changing Light of the World to declare, "Lord, I believe," and worship Him.

THIRTEEN

THE DEATH CONQUEROR

It was Super Bowl Sunday, and after our morning service, we were at home, getting ready to have some guests over to watch the big game with us. About an hour before kickoff, our phones chimed with a text from our son, who lives about forty miles away from us: "You may or may not soon hear the news, but an airplane seems to have just exploded and crashed in the air above our house. We are fine. Not that you should worry, but just thought you should know."

Telling parents not to worry is, of course, futile. We tried to contact Stephen, and when we couldn't, we immediately turned on the television to see the reports. Later conversations revealed that Stephen had heard a midair explosion, seen a small plane going down, and had heard the crash, just blocks from his home. His three children, hearing all this, had rushed to find him. As they stood in their back yard, the black smoke rising from houses incinerated by the crash was perilously close. Sadly, four people simply going about their lives in the apparent safety of their home lost their lives, as did the pilot of the plane. All this happened about two blocks from my son's home.

It was impossible not to give thanks that it hadn't been them and their house. But it could have been, and the feeling of sadness for those who had no way of knowing their lives were about to end was deep. Sympathy for families left behind made it all a very sobering experience. Of all the ways that death might come to someone I love, a scenario so bizarre and tragic had never entered my mind.

Death always comes as the great intruder. Thankfully, it doesn't usually intrude in such an unexpected and apparently random way as it did that day. But, however it comes, it interrupts our lives and shatters the status quo. Even when it is expected, and perhaps even desired, it barges its way into our lives. More often, it snatches away people we cherish, mocks plans we have made, and darkens our future. We live in a time of unrivaled medical advancements and technological innovations, causing us to believe that we should expect to live longer lives free from the plagues and diseases that have haunted human history. But the onset of the coronavirus epidemic was an unwelcome reminder of our frailty. After all, even at their best, medical science and modern technology can only postpone the inevitable, not cancel it. Death will always have the final word.

Or will it? The central conviction of the Christian faith is that, through His death and resurrection, the Lord Jesus has made death profoundly different. Death is still a great enemy, but it doesn't have the final word; the Lord Jesus does. He displayed in His own life a power over death, and by His resurrection He opened a door to a new future for His people. In one of His final miracles, He laid the foundation for a new hope that can look death squarely in the eye, and face it with deep confidence, even in the midst of profound sorrow. Because of our risen Lord, we view death with tear-filled but hope-filled eyes, with resilient anticipation, not stoic resignation.

Three times in His earthly ministry, the Lord Jesus raised someone from the dead. In chapter 8, we considered His raising of Jairus's daughter. Luke records for us His dramatic interruption of a funeral in the little village of Nain, where He raised a grieving widow's only son (Luke 7:11–17). While we speak of these as resurrections, they were actually restorations from death to life, since each of these people would die once again. Still, they are wonderful anticipations of the resurrection of the Lord Jesus, with its promise that believers in Him will receive a resurrection body that will never again be subject to death and sickness. As the apostle Paul writes, "But our citizenship is in heaven, and from it we await a Savior, the Lord Jesus Christ, who will transform our lowly body to be like his glorious body, by the power that enables him even to subject all things to himself" (Philippians 3:20–21).

The most dramatic of these restorations to life is the miracle that we are going to consider in this chapter. The exact timing of this event isn't entirely clear. What is clear is that Jesus's confrontation with the Jewish leaders, aroused by His healing of the man born blind that we considered in chapter 12, had made it very dangerous for Him to remain in the region of Jerusalem. So He most probably returned to Galilee for a time, then, at some point returned south. He went away to a location east of the Jordan River, near one of John the Baptist's baptismal sites (John 10:39–41), probably just a few miles from the city of Jericho.

Death, the Great Intruder: "Your Friend Lazarus Is Sick"

Now a certain man was ill, Lazarus of Bethany, the village of Mary and her sister Martha. It was Mary who anointed the Lord with ointment and wiped his feet with her hair, whose brother Lazarus was ill. So the sisters sent to him, saying, "Lord, he whom you love is ill." But when Jesus heard it he said, "This illness does not lead to death. It is for the glory of God, so that the Son of God may be glorified through it."

Now Jesus loved Martha and her sister and Lazarus. So, when he heard that Lazarus was ill, he stayed two days longer in the place where he was. Then after this he said to the disciples, "Let us go to Judea again." The disciples said to him, "Rabbi, the Jews were just now seeking to stone you, and are you going there again?" Jesus answered, "Are there not twelve hours in the day? If anyone walks in the day, he does not stumble, because he sees the light of this world. But if anyone walks in the night, he stumbles, because the light is not in him." After saying these things, he said to them, "Our friend Lazarus has fallen asleep, but I go to awaken him." The disciples said to him, "Lord, if he has fallen asleep, he will recover." Now Jesus had spoken of his death, but they thought that he meant taking rest in sleep. Then Jesus told them plainly, "Lazarus has died, and for your sake I am glad that I was not there, so that you may believe. But let us go to him." So Thomas, called the Twin, said to his fellow disciples, "Let us also go, that we may die with him." (John 11:1–16)

John 11 is one of the richest chapters in the Gospels and certainly deserves more attention than we can give it in this chapter. But we shouldn't pass too quickly over this introductory section, since it is loaded with significance. Once again, Jesus takes us by surprise. Just when we think we can predict what He will do, He does something very different.

The family of Lazarus, Martha, and Mary had become very special to Jesus. They lived in Bethany, a village on the Mount of Olives, a short walk from Jerusalem. Theirs was a home where

Jesus had enjoyed refreshment, friendship, and hospitality (Luke 10:38–42), and His links with the family were strong. John goes out of his way to underline the mutual affection they enjoyed: "he whom you love is ill" (John 11:3); "Jesus loved Martha and her sister and Lazarus" (v. 5); "our friend Lazarus" (v. 11); "See how he loved him!" (v. 36). So, when Lazarus came down with a life-threatening illness, the sisters knew exactly what to do. They immediately dispatched a messenger with the news: "Lord, he whom you love is ill." Obviously they didn't intend this as a news bulletin. It was a cry for help. They were utterly convinced that Jesus would drop whatever He was doing, come as quickly as possible, and rescue their brother from his approaching death.

That's not what happened. John puts it in the most provocative way possible: "Now Jesus loved Martha and her sister and Lazarus. So, when he heard that Lazarus was ill, he stayed two days longer in the place where he was." He did what!? What kind of sense does that make? He loved him so much that He stayed? And whatever could He mean by telling the messenger, "This illness does not lead to death. It is for the glory of God, so that the Son of God may be glorified through it"? We know that Lazarus did, in fact, die. What did that mean?

Behind His seeming indifference to this family's plight stood a higher purpose. His delay was not motivated by indifference to their sorrow. Nor was it due to intimidation from the Jews, even though Jesus had death threats waiting for Him in Jerusalem. Certainly Thomas recognized that going would be dangerous (v. 16), but that wasn't Jesus's motive for staying. After all, He did ultimately go.

Jesus was indicating that His delay was for important reasons. First, it was going to be the means of displaying His glory, as well as His Father's glory. Lazarus's illness would only result in a temporary death, and then in an even greater life. The sufferings of Lazarus and his sisters would provide a platform for the glory of God to be revealed. Further, as Jesus said to His disciples, "For your sake I am glad that I was not there, so that you may believe." Glad that Lazarus had died? That sounds preposterous, unless we understand that the Lord was completely sovereign over what was happening, and very intentional in providing what the disciples would need in the coming years.

Mysterious as Jesus's delay was, it was not purposeless. That is always the case. The Lord who promises to be with us as the Good Shepherd in the valley of the shadow of death has purposes beyond our understanding. In later years, I suspect that Lazarus and his sisters probably looked back to say, "It was really hard, but I'm so glad He didn't come right away. Think of what we would have missed." It is wise, not foolish, to trust the character and promises of our ever-faithful Shepherd, even when we can make no sense of His apparent absence when we need and want Him most. There is an important truth here: *We tend to interpret God's love by circumstances; we need to interpret circumstances in the light of His unfailing love, His all-wise purposes, and His unfailing promises.*

Death Raises Ultimate Questions: "I Am the Resurrection and the Life"

> Now when Jesus came, he found that Lazarus had already been in the tomb four days. Bethany was near Jerusalem, about two miles off, and many of the Jews had come to Martha and Mary to console them concerning their brother. So when Martha heard that Jesus was coming, she went and met him, but Mary remained seated in the house. Martha said to Jesus, "Lord, if you had been here, my brother would not have died. But even now I know that whatever you ask from God, God will give you." Jesus said to her, "Your brother

will rise again." Martha said to him, "I know that he will rise again in the resurrection on the last day." Jesus said to her, "I am the resurrection and the life. Whoever believes in me, though he die, yet shall he live, and everyone who lives and believes in me shall never die. Do you believe this?" She said to him, "Yes, Lord; I believe that you are the Christ, the Son of God, who is coming into the world." (John 11:17–27)

Jewish custom called for burials to take place on the same day as death, and when Jesus finally arrived, He was told that Lazarus had been buried four days earlier. This, by the way, indicates that, had He come when summoned, He would not have arrived before Lazarus's death. There can also now be no doubt that Lazarus was really dead. There was a Jewish folk belief that a soul would linger near a body for three days before it left. But by the fourth day His body would already be decomposing, as Martha will complain in verse 39.

Jewish custom also called friends and family to comfort the bereaved with their presence, support, and shared grief. So, when Jesus arrived, the sisters were surrounded by companions who had come to sit *shiva* with them. Some were neighbors, and many had made the short walk from Jerusalem.

Someone brought word to the sisters that Jesus had arrived and was waiting some distance off, almost certainly to provide an opportunity for a somewhat private conversation. Hearing the news, Martha rushed out to meet Him with her questions.

That was something of a breach of custom. Sympathizers came to the bereaved, but Martha wasn't waiting on formalities. While she was glad to see Him, she was also hurt, confused, and even angry. Why hadn't He come sooner? He would have made such a difference. Her faith in Jesus was real; her confusion about Him obvious: "Lord, if you had been here!" (v. 21).

The implied "Lord, if only" with which she met Jesus is revealing. She acknowledged His special identity with the word *Lord* but also admitted her bewilderment with both a wish and a complaint. Her faith in Him was real—"my brother would not have died" (v. 21)—but her heart was wounded. She was glad to see Jesus but also full of questions. Death is often filled with *if onlys*—"If only *I* (or *he* or *they* or *you*) . . ." Questions bombard our minds and steal our peace. Yet Martha was convinced that Jesus could still make a difference: "Whatever you ask from God, God will give you" (v. 22). What she had in mind isn't at all clear. From what followed, it seems obvious that she had no expectation that Lazarus would be restored to life.

The Lord's initial response was to assure Martha that her brother would rise again. She believed in the resurrection of the righteous at the end of time and instantly assumed that this was what Jesus had in mind. "I know that he will rise again in the resurrection on the last day" (v. 24). Death had not ended his existence. She knew this, but that belief didn't meet the immediate need of her heart. She was orthodox in her theology but also struggling to make it personal and find real peace. We don't know much about the personal lives of Mary and Martha, but if Lazarus was the only protective male in their family, the sisters' future would be very uncertain without him. Martha had a textbook orthodoxy, but she lacked a deep inner confidence about how that could affect her life here and now. In that, she is a mirror of what many of us feel at the grave of a loved one.

The Lord's response is one of the greatest declarations to be found in the Scriptures. He didn't give Mary an explanation, but a jaw-dropping assertion. She believed that God would raise her brother. But Jesus claimed, "I am the resurrection and the life. Whoever believes in me, though he die, yet shall he live, and everyone who lives and believes in me shall never die" (vv. 25–26). Jesus is resurrection personified. He does not merely "do" resurrection: "I am the resurrection and the life." This is the fifth of seven "I am" affirmations that Jesus makes about himself in John's gospel.[1] Jesus was pointing Martha to "Who," not "What." Hope is found not in the fact of the resurrection, but in the person of the Resurrected One. He is Lord of, and over, life and death.

That Jesus is "the resurrection" points to the physical body. He will bring about the resurrection of the body, transformed and made imperishable and glorious. That Jesus is "the life" refers to spiritual life, the life of God himself. A believer in Him will live, even though he dies. There are, in fact, two kinds of death—physical and spiritual—and the Lord Jesus is the answer to both. *Because of Christ, death does not mean the termination of life, or even an interruption of life, but a transformation of our experience of life, from the temporal to the eternal.*

It is an astonishing promise, made to "whoever believes in me" (v. 25). He gives unending life and promises bodily resurrection to those who entrust themselves to Him.

These words could be dismissed as the rantings of a deranged mind, were it not for what followed, first the raising of Lazarus, and then the even more awesome victory of the Lord Jesus over His own death on Easter Sunday morning. The death and resurrection of Jesus made everything different, especially death. Now, through Him, where there is death, there is triumphant hope.

Jesus concluded His declaration with a direct question to Martha, and to us as well: "Do you believe this?" (v. 26). For a moment, Martha could see, through her tear-filled eyes, who really was standing in front of her: "Yes, Lord; I believe that you are the Christ, the Son of God, who is coming into the world" (v. 27). It is a wonderful declaration, with an important twist. Martha was declaring her faith not simply in Jesus's claim, but in Jesus himself, as God's Messiah. She believes *Him*, not merely *His message*. Within minutes, Martha would have even more reason for entrusting her-self to Him.

Death Submits to a Greater Power: God's Glory on Display

When she had said this, she went and called her sister Mary, saying in private, "The Teacher is here and is calling for you." And when she heard it, she rose quickly and went to him. Now Jesus had not yet come into the village, but was still in the place where Martha had met him. When the Jews who were with her in the house, consoling her, saw Mary rise quickly and go out, they followed her, supposing that she was going to the tomb to weep there. Now when Mary came to where Jesus was and saw him, she fell at his feet, saying to him, "Lord, if you had been here, my brother would not have died." When Jesus saw her weeping, and the Jews who had come with her also weeping, he was deeply moved in his spirit and greatly troubled. And he said, "Where have you laid him?" They said to him, "Lord, come and see." Jesus wept. So the Jews said, "See how he loved him!" But some of them said, "Could not he who opened the eyes of the blind man also have kept this man from dying?"

Then Jesus, deeply moved again, came to the tomb. It was a cave, and a stone lay against it. Jesus said, "Take away the stone." Martha, the sister of the dead man, said to him, "Lord, by this time there will be an odor, for he has been dead four days." Jesus said to her, "Did I not tell you that if you believed you would see the glory of God?" So they took away the stone. And Jesus lifted up his eyes and said, "Father, I thank you that you have heard me. I knew that you always hear me, but I said this on account of the people standing around, that they may believe that you sent me." When he had said these things, he cried out with a loud voice, "Lazarus, come out." The man who had died came out, his hands and feet bound with linen strips, and his face wrapped with a cloth. Jesus said to them, "Unbind him, and let him go." (John 11:28–44)

At this point, Martha felt the need to alert Mary to Jesus's presence. Mary's response was characteristic of her—rushing to Jesus and throwing herself at His feet, weeping. Mary's personality was different than Martha's—expressive and emotional, a feeler in contrast to Martha's doer. Their sorrow was the same, as were their words: "Lord, if you had been here, my brother would not have died" (John 11:32). Yet their needs were different. If Martha needed answers, Mary needs emotional support. And the Lord Jesus responded with a remarkable mixture of emotions. With eloquent brevity, John writes, "Jesus wept" (v. 35). He grieved with her, identifying with her heartache. As fully man, He entered deeply into her sorrow. It is a moment to be cherished by Christians. The writer of Hebrews reminds us that "we do not have a high priest who is unable to sympathize with our weaknesses" (Hebrews 4:15). Death hurts, and our Lord wept at its impact on those He loved.

And yet we also read that when He saw the other mourners who were there, "he was deeply moved in his spirit and greatly troubled" (John 11:33). The startling thing is that the word translated "deeply moved" usually connotes feelings of anger or indignation. Some have suggested His anger was caused by these other mourners invading their privacy. That hardly seems likely. Others suggest it was due to the hypocrisy of some who were there, enemies of Jesus. But it is more likely that His indignation was directed at the destructiveness of sin and death. This was not the way things were supposed to be. Death is an enemy He would meet and defeat at the cross. It is right to be angry at death. Death is not the way it's supposed to be, and Christians are not called to stoic resignation in its presence.

When the entourage finally arrived at Lazarus's tomb, a cave covered by a stone, Jesus suddenly shocked them with a strange but authoritative command: "Take away the stone" (v. 39). Despite her deep affection and respect for Him, Martha couldn't restrain her protest at what seemed both disgusting and an act of desecration. Why would Jesus want to see the body? "Lord, he's been dead four days—his remains will be putrid." But her objection was restrained by the Lord's rejoinder: "Did I not tell you that if you believed you would see the glory of God?" (v. 40). And so they agreed, if reluctantly, to His audacious request; the stone was removed.

For one of the only times recorded in the Gospels, the Lord prayed in connection with one of His miracles. But it wasn't a request for His Father's help. Rather, it was an act of public thanksgiving. Then He uttered an abrupt command: "Lazarus, come out" (v. 43). What good does it do to command a dead man to do anything? But what the Lord commands, the Lord enables. Lazarus played no part in his raising. Jesus spoke; the dead man heard and responded, because the Lord enabled him to do so. When the enshrouded, shuffling figure emerged from the darkness, Jesus gave a second command—this time not to Lazarus, but to the astonished stone movers: "Unbind him, and let him go" (v. 44). The Death Conqueror had spoken, and death had surrendered its prey.

That is the end of the story, and yet only the beginning. In the verses that follow, we learn that many of those who witnessed this miracle became believing followers of Jesus. What other reasonable response could there be? But those who chose to be blind refused to see, no matter how clearly the sign pointed to the supernatural identity of the Lord Jesus. The Jewish leaders, hearing the story, would not repent. Rather, they redoubled their determination to be rid of Jesus. In fact, when the persuasiveness of the evidence drew increased numbers to Jesus, they conspired to kill not only Jesus (v. 53) but Lazarus as well (12:9–11). Sadly, the miracle of Lazarus only increased their rebellion, clear evidence of the hardness of human hearts apart from the gracious intervention of God.

The raising of Lazarus from the dead is, in every conceivable way, an amazing event. It was a display of the Lord's hidden glory, the "glory as of the only Son from the Father" (1:14). Jesus had said that through His friend's illness, He would be glorified (11:4), and so He was. That glory was resident in Jesus. And yet, Lazarus's resuscitation was only a temporary resurrection; he would die again. It was, however, an anticipation of the Lord's resurrection, in which He would be raised qualitatively different, with an imperishable body, the prototype of the body all true believers will receive at the return of the One who is the resurrection and the life (1 Corinthians 15:51–53; 1 Thessalonians 4:15–17). And the raising of Lazarus is confirmation of the Lord's promise that the one who believes in Him will never die, but that to be "away from the body" is to be "at home with the Lord" (2 Corinthians 5:8; Philippians 1:23). Resurrection and eternal life are not the promise for those who are good enough to earn it or receive it. They are the gifts of our Savior, who died and rose again so *that those who trust in Him might receive them.*

FOURTEEN

"MY LORD AND MY GOD"

"Why do any of you consider it incredible that God raises the dead?" (Acts 26:8 CSB). The question was posed by the apostle Paul as he stood before the Roman governor Festus and King Herod Agrippa II, the great-grandson of Herod the Great. But Paul wasn't really arguing about what God could do. His concern was about what God had done. As Festus had told Agrippa the previous day, he was speaking specifically about "a certain Jesus, a dead man Paul claimed to be alive" (25:19 CSB). We have, in a sense, circled around to the question that began this book, "Can we even believe in miracles?" If there is a God, of course we can. But the most important question remains: "Did Jesus of Nazareth rise from the dead?" Because if He did, that changes everything. We began the book by saying that the central Christian miracle is the incarnation, that God became man in the person of Christ. But we can only know the incarnation is true if the resurrection is indeed true. If Jesus died and remained dead, as all humans do, then why would we suppose that He was somehow different from every other person who has ever lived? So the question of the reality of the resurrection of the Lord Jesus is both unavoidable and critical.

The Christian faith rises or falls on the physical resurrection of the Lord Jesus Christ. That is why Paul declares it to be "of first importance . . . that Christ died for our sins in accordance with the Scriptures, that he was buried, that he was raised the third day in accordance with the Scriptures, and that he appeared to Cephas, and then to the twelve" (1 Corinthians 15:3–5). Apart from the resurrection, we could be sure that He died, but we would never, and could never, know that He is the Christ, whose death was for our sins, not His own. No wonder Paul goes on to say that "if Christ has not been raised, your faith is futile and you are still in your sins" (v. 17).

All of the miracles we have considered to this point have been clearly and directly performed by the Lord Jesus on His own authority, in virtue of His own power. But you will notice that Paul tells us that "he *was* raised" (v. 4, emphasis added), obviously referring to the work of God the Father in bringing Him back to life. That is the most common way the New Testament describes the resurrection: it was God the Father's vindication of His Son. Yet, at the same time, Jesus speaks of His own role in His resurrection. Early in His ministry, He declared rather cryptically, while standing in Herod's magnificent temple, "Destroy this temple, and in three days I will raise it up" (John 2:19). When the Jewish leaders heard this audacious claim from Jesus, they mocked His pretentious claim. But John clarifies the Lord's meaning and its significance: "He was speaking about the temple of his body. When therefore he was raised from the dead, his disciples remembered that he had said this, and they believed the Scripture and the word that Jesus had spoken" (vv. 21–22). "I will raise it. . . . He was raised." Somehow, He was active in the events of resurrection morning, not just acted upon. That is even clearer in a profoundly compact statement found later in John's gospel: "For this reason the Father loves me, because I lay down my life that I may take it up again. No one takes it from me, but I lay it down of my own accord. I have authority to lay it down, and I have authority to take it up again. This charge I have received from my Father" (John 10:17–18). In contrast to Lazarus, Jesus is the agent of His own resurrection, in concert with His Father.

My life was profoundly changed when I came to the conviction that Jesus really had risen from the dead on Resurrection Sunday morning. I love to return to the reasons for that conviction regularly, but for our purposes, as we come to the end of our journey through the miracles of our Lord, I want to turn our attention rather briefly to that history-transforming day, as John describes it for us in John 20.

Bad News: "They Have Taken the Lord"

> Now on the first day of the week Mary Magdalene came to the tomb early, while it was still dark, and saw that the stone had been taken away from the tomb. So she ran and went to Simon Peter and the other disciple, the one whom Jesus loved, and said to them, "They have taken the Lord out of the tomb, and we do not know where they have laid him." (John 20:1–2)

One thing is clear: As the first Easter Sunday dawned, not a single one of His followers expected to see Jesus alive ever again. Even though He had warned them of this very thing, their minds simply couldn't grasp the idea of a crucified Messiah. And they had even less ability to imagine that He could rise again. So, while they had heard His words, they had repressed His message. All they wanted now was to remember and honor Him as best way they could, so they could move on with their lives. That desire led a group of grieving women to rise very early on the day after the Sabbath to journey to His tomb, where they were determined to pay their final respects to Him.

When they set out, they had no doubt about what they were going to encounter. They had been witnesses at the cross, when Jesus had breathed His last, and they had watched as a soldier pushed a sword into His side to confirm that He was dead. They had watched through grief-filled eyes as His body was removed from that cross. Normally, the Romans would leave a crucified victim's body to rot on a cross, to perpetuate the horrific consequences of offending Roman authority. However, not wishing to inflame Jewish sensibilities, the Romans had chosen simply to remove victims' bodies and dispose of them in common graves. But, in Jesus's case, due to the intervention of high-ranking Jewish citizens, Pilate had allowed Jesus to be buried in a private tomb. These women had stayed to the very end, watching the hasty preparations for burial, and observing as the tomb was secured by a large stone, sealed and stamped with an official Roman insignia, and guarded by a military cohort. Therefore, their main concern on this early morning was how they could get into a tomb sealed in such a layered way, so as to accomplish their self-appointed task of treating His remains with the dignity and respect they believed He deserved.

There was a group of women involved in this project (Matthew 28:1–2; Mark 16:1; Luke 23:55–24:1), but John focuses our attention on only one of them, Mary Magdalene. She was a woman whose life had been changed through the Lord Jesus. Plagued by seven demons (Luke 8:2), she had been completely delivered by Him. As a result, she had become His devoted follower, joining the group that had traveled with Him from Galilee, only to be heartbroken by the stunning events that took place during the Pass-over celebration.

Now, as she made her way through the gloom of a new dawn, unspeakably heavy of heart, she only wished for one thing: the opportunity to show her gratitude one last time to the man who had forever changed her life. But it was not to be! As she drew close enough to see where Jesus had been entombed, her grief suddenly turned into shock, despair, and growing anger. The stone had been rolled away! And when she rushed to the open cave to look in, she found the tomb was empty and the body was gone! She knew that she hadn't gone to the wrong tomb. How could she ever forget this place? The corpse of Jesus of Nazareth had vanished.

Mary's response is very significant. Her first reaction wasn't "He is risen!" That didn't occur to her. No, her response was "He's been stolen!" She will repeat that declaration three times in John's account. This seemed the final indignity of all that had occurred over the last few days in the travesty of justice that had led to Jesus's execution. How else could anyone explain this un-thinkable violation of propriety and breach of security? Either the Jewish leaders or the Romans had not been content with merely killing Jesus; they apparently wanted to erase any trace of His ex-istence. That seemed the only possible conclusion, and it made her both anxious and angry.

Her response was instinctive: she had to tell the men. She turned away from the tomb, and rushed to the place where the disciples were meeting. Entering, she blurted the news: "They have taken the Lord out of the tomb, and we do not know where they have laid him" (John 20:2). We must not miss the significance of this. The empty tomb in and of itself did not produce faith in the followers of Jesus. Rather, it aroused fear, confusion, anger, and despair. Neither Mary nor the disciples who heard her report saw in this the answer to the Lord's promise that He would take up His life again. As morning dawned, the empty tomb seemed to be very bad news.

Strange News: The Puzzling Discovery of a Not-Quite-Empty Tomb

So Peter went out with the other disciple, and they were going toward the tomb. Both of them were running together, but the other disciple outran Peter and reached the tomb first. And stooping to look in, he saw the linen cloths lying there, but he did not go in. Then Simon Peter came, following him, and went into the tomb. He saw the linen cloths lying there, and the face cloth, which had been on Jesus' head, not lying with the linen cloths but folded up in a place by itself. Then the other disciple, who had reached the tomb first, also went in, and he saw and believed; for as yet they did not understand the Scripture, that he must rise from the dead. Then the disciples went back to their homes. (John 20:3–10)

Mary's announcement rang an alarm bell for the disciples. Could this really be the case, or was she just confused? This was too important a matter simply to take her word for it. If the authorities had done this to Jesus, their lives were also in danger. So Peter and John (who regularly disguises his identity in the gospel as "the one whom Jesus loved") immediately set off to see for themselves. John outran Peter on this occasion, arriving first at the tomb. It is important to observe once again that no one had any doubt about the location of Jesus's burial place. Some have foolishly suggested that, in their grief, everyone forgot where Jesus was actually buried, and so they all went to the wrong tomb, found it empty, and conjured up the entire resurrection story. Such people must have never buried a loved one! I have very little trouble finding the graves of my daughter or my parents in crowded cemeteries, even years after their deaths.

John's natural reticence made him stop at the entrance of the tomb. The tomb was a cave, or was at least cavelike, with a small opening and a larger burial chamber. As John stooped to look inside, we are told that "he saw the linen cloths lying there" (John 20:5). That in itself was strange. Why, if the body had been taken by the authorities, would they go to the trouble of unwrapping it? Or, if it was the work of grave robbers, how had they dealt with the Roman guard, and what possible motive could they have for unwrapping the body? Whatever the case, the wrappings were there, but the corpse wasn't!

As John was pondering all this, Peter reached the tomb, and with his typical boldness, pushed past John to enter the burial chamber itself. He saw what John had seen and more: "He saw the linen cloths lying there, and the face cloth, which had been on Jesus' head, not lying with the linen cloths but folded up in a place by itself" (vv. 6–7). We need to pay careful attention to this description, since more is being communicated than we might at first imagine.

John has told us in the previous chapter that those who prepared Jesus for burial "took the body of Jesus and bound it in linen cloths with the spices, as is the burial custom of the Jews" (John 19:40). It is these cloths that Peter sees, but they are described as "lying there." Linen cloths were expensive, and in this case they were filled with valuable spices. Why would they have been left behind? But Peter now also saw what John had been unable to see: "the face cloth folded up in a place by itself." This cloth had obviously been dealt with carefully, not hastily or casually. As Peter pondered all of this, he also tried to make sense of it all. The presence and position of the grave clothes made no sense, if either robbers or conspirators had been behind the disappearance of Jesus's body.

Some moments later, John entered to stand alongside Peter. "He saw and believed" (John 20:8). Interestingly, he makes a subtle change of language from his description of Peter. Peter "saw" physically the linen cloths lying on the floor of the tomb," but John "saw" (using a different Greek word for "see"). John not only viewed the cloths; he was also given insight and understanding into what the condition of the grave cloths meant. Jesus's body hadn't been stolen; he had risen! Some suggest that the condition of the grave cloths indicated that Jesus's body had passed through those cloths, leaving them in the shape of His corpse. We cannot be sure that is the case, although it is a possibility. Regardless, John recognized that the grave clothes were silent witnesses to a stunning miracle. His words here are his personal testimony to resurrection faith: He came to faith in the risen Christ because of what he saw as incontrovertible evidence that a resurrection had occurred. He now knew fully that, because He had risen, "Jesus is the Christ, the Son of God" (John 20:31).

We are not told what Peter's immediate response was. He was carrying in his heart deep guilt for having denied his Lord. Luke tells us that he returned from the tomb "marveling at what had happened" (Luke 24:12). Undeniably, something remarkable had happened, but the certainty that John had gained still eluded him.

Great News: "I Have Seen the Lord"

But Mary stood weeping outside the tomb, and as she wept she stooped to look into the tomb. And she saw two angels in white, sitting where the body of Jesus had lain, one at the head and one at the feet. They said to her, "Woman, why are you weeping?" She said to them, "They have taken away my Lord, and I do not know where they have laid him." Having said this, she turned around and saw Jesus standing, but she did not know that it was Jesus. Jesus said to her, "Woman, why are you weeping? Whom are you seeking?" Supposing him to be the gardener, she said to him, "Sir, if you have carried him away, tell me where you have laid him, and I will take him away." Jesus said to her, "Mary." She turned and said to him in Aramaic, "Rabboni!" (which means Teacher). Jesus said to her, "Do not cling to me, for I have not yet ascended to the Father; but go to my brothers and say to them, 'I am ascending to my Father and your Father, to my God and your God.'" Mary Magdalene went and announced to the disciples, "I have seen the Lord"—and that he had said these things to her. (John 20:11–18)

It is of great importance that the early Christians did not believe in the resurrection because they had found an empty tomb. That the tomb was empty on Easter Sunday morning is a stubborn and important fact that resists all attempts to dismiss it. Jesus's body was not discarded and eaten by dogs. People didn't all have amnesia and forget its proper location. The disciples didn't steal the body. They couldn't have, given the presence of the guard, and wouldn't have, given their complete lack of expectation that Jesus would rise again. Still, it was not the indirect evidence of Jesus's absent body that inspired resurrection faith, but the tangible presence of the living Christ. They believed in the resurrection not only because they saw their living Lord but because their hands touched His body. He was no phantom!

The first to do so was Mary Magdalene. Although we will not engage this passage in detail, we must not dismiss its importance. Although John had believed because of the empty tomb, Mary hadn't. His body may have been gone, but she couldn't stay away from the last place where she had a connection with the Lord she loved. In her despair, she returned to linger by His tomb, hoping for any clue about what might have happened to His body. Like a magnet, it drew her. The empty tomb was now the closest she would ever come to everything she had believed in and hoped for. Even the presence of angels brought her no relief. All she could do was complain to them: "They have taken away my Lord" (v. 13).

In fact, her eyes were so filled with tears and her heart so filled with grief that when Jesus himself stood before her, she failed to recognize Him. She knew He was dead, so whoever this man was, he couldn't be Him. She may have thought, If this man is here by the tomb, perhaps he was complicit in what has happened: "Sir, if you have carried him away, tell me where you have laid him, and I will take him away" (v. 15).

It is remarkable that, in a world where women were not considered reliable enough to give valid testimony in courts of law, Jesus deliberately sought out a woman to be the first witness of His resurrection. Dorothy Sayers famously said that women were the last at the cross and the first at the tomb. And now a woman—not Peter, James, or John, His closest allies—became the first to encounter the risen Christ. And not just any woman, but a woman with an unsavory past! With one word, Jesus changed everything: "Mary" (v. 16). I have often thought that if I could choose any moment to be a witness of gospel events, this one would be high on my list. I would love to hear the love and grace with which Jesus spoke the name of that heartbroken woman. And I would love to hear her shout of instant recognition: "Rabboni!" (v. 16), as she threw herself at His feet, desperately clinging to Him, as if He were a figment of her imagination that might vanish at any moment. But He was really there, and in an instant all of human history was changed. She had seen the Lord, risen from the dead!

So she became the first in a string of eyewitnesses to the risen Christ. John goes on to tell us of two specific events. Later that day, the disciples gathered together, both because the Jewish leaders still represented a threat to them, but most of all because of the mysterious reports they had received that some of their number had seen Jesus. Other women had encountered Jesus with Mary (Matthew 28:1–10). It was reported that Peter had apparently seen Him too (Luke 24:34; 1 Corinthians 15:5), though that first meeting is not recorded in the Gospels. Even as they were gathering, two disciples arrived from the village of Emmaus to share how they had been met by the risen Lord as they traveled on the road, an encounter that had turned despair into delight. The room must have been filled with excited but puzzled chatter. Then, suddenly, "Jesus came and stood among them and said to them, 'Peace be with you'" (John 20:19). It was a never-to-be-forgotten moment as "he showed them his hands and his side." There was no question this was Jesus, bearing the wounds of His crucifixion as He did. He was the same Jesus, but not really. After all, He had suddenly appeared in a locked room, without using the door! His was a new kind of body. And so, in one of the great understatements in the Gospels, John declares, "Then the disciples were glad when they saw the Lord" (v. 20).

More appearances were to follow, but John passes over those to describe another meeting, exactly one week later, in the same room. The disciple Thomas had been absent the previous week, but he had heard the reports from his fellow disciples. To him, they seemed impossible, too good to be true, the projections of fevered imaginations. During that intervening week, they kept excitedly repeating the same story: "We have seen the Lord!" Thomas wasn't buying it. We speak today of post-traumatic stress disorder. When the nails went into Jesus's body, they had also gone into Thomas's soul, leaving him distressed and disillusioned. Dead people just don't return to life. He loved his friends; they'd shared so much together. But he couldn't, and wouldn't, follow them into this journey of wishful thinking: "Unless I see in his hands the mark of the nails, and place my finger into the mark of the nails, and place my hand into his side, I will never believe" (v. 25). His heart and his mind were nailed shut.

Still, he loved his friends enough to be with them that night, behind locked doors. In a repeat of the previous Sunday, "Jesus came and stood among them and said, 'Peace be with you'" (v. 26). We can only imagine Thomas's feelings at that moment, when the Lord Jesus turned directly toward him. Somehow He knew about Thomas's emphatic skepticism. But His words were not words of rebuke for his doubts, but rather an invitation that filled exactly the conditions he had declared: "Put your finger here, and see my hands; and put out your hand, and place it in my side. Do not disbelieve, but believe" (v. 27). The Lord Jesus does not resist investigation; He invites it. Genuine faith is, as we've noted, not a call to the beliefs of the gullible without evidence, but deeply rooted trust on the basis of overwhelming evidence.

Thomas's response was immediate and profound. He did believe. How could he not? But he not only believed, he worshipped: "My Lord and my God!" (v. 28). We are not told whether he even bothered carrying out his tests. The evidence was clear: this was the same Jesus he had followed as a disciple, the same Jesus who had been crucified and buried. But He was far more. Thomas instantly realized that whatever categories he had previously used to describe the Lord were completely inadequate to describe the One before whom he instinctively bowed. The risen Jesus is Lord and God of all who put their faith in Him. He is, in fact, King of kings and Lord of lords, before whom all will bow. "My Lord and my God" is a confession not only of faith but of submission and worship.

With the possible exception of the miracle at the wedding in Cana, Thomas had witnessed all the miracles we have studied in this book. But it was the resurrection of Jesus that finally helped him understand who the Lord Jesus fully was. *The resurrection confirms the identity of the Lord Jesus,* making it clear that the risen Lord is the eternal Lord. He didn't just raise the dead; He overpowered death, having given His life only to take it up again. So Christians are those who find themselves at the feet of Jesus alongside Thomas, worshipping and hailing Him as our Lord and God. This is not the wishful declaration of naïveté but the wholehearted proclamation of certainty.

The resurrection also transforms our understanding of the cross. Late on Friday afternoon, the crucifixion of Jesus was vivid evidence of a catastrophic defeat. Jesus died at the hands of sinful men and corrupt leaders. Evil had won. But on Sunday morning, the cross looked entirely different. Jesus's death was not the victory of unjust political actors, but the victory of a righteous God. The Lord had died, not as the penalty for His sins but as the payment for ours, in fulfillment of Scripture's promises.

The resurrection of the Savior also marked the inauguration of a deeper and richer relationship to God. When the Lord told Mary Magdalene to go to the disciples, He commissioned her to "go to my brothers and say to them, 'I am ascending to my Father and your Father, to my God and your God'" (v. 17). This is language foreign to the Old Testament, language that announces the establishment of the new covenant, confirmed by the sending of the Holy Spirit on the day of Pentecost to indwell all those who entrust themselves to King Jesus. Through the risen Christ, we have been brought into the family of God, adopted as sons and daughters by virtue of our relationship with the Lord Jesus, and given assurance of an eternal home with Him.

The resurrection furthermore guarantees the promises of Jesus. Only the living Lord can promise us, "Whoever believes in me, though he die, yet shall he live" (11:25), or, "In my Father's house are many rooms. If it were not so, would I have told you that I go to prepare a place for you? And if I go and prepare a place for you, I will come again and will take you to myself, that where I am you may be also" (14:2–3). In the words of Paul, "All the promises of God find their Yes in him" (2 Corinthians 1:20).

By His resurrection, our risen Lord also opens a new view of our mission in life. Among His first words to Mary Magdalene were "Go to my brothers" (John 20:17), and Mary went, carrying the glad news of the resurrection. On that first Easter night, the risen Lord commissioned His disciples with a new view of the world: "As the Father has sent me, even so I am sending you" (v. 21). He said this to men who had locked themselves in a room because they were afraid of the people who had crucified their Master. But the grave could not hold Him, and the news of His resurrection is too good to keep secret! The presence of the risen Christ changes doubters into believers; people once plagued by fear become pro-claimers of the gospel, marked by courage and faith.

CONCLUSION

—ᴍ—

Jesus worked miracles, but He wasn't a "wonder-worker," at least not in the way we conventionally use that term. As we have seen, His miracles were not stage-managed performances or self-serving events designed to astonish and arouse a popular following. Just to choose one occasion, after the feeding of the five thousand, we are told that "perceiving then that they were about to come and take him by force to make him king, Jesus withdrew again to the mountain by himself" (John 6:15). Miracles were undeniably a central part of His ministry, and they did arouse amazement and public interest. But, as we have seen, they also aroused fear, confusion, controversy, and murderous opposition. The same miracles that caused some to say, "He has done all things well" (Mark 7:37), led others to make "plans to put him to death" (John 11:53).

In all of His deeds, there isn't a trace of any jaw-dropping supernatural stunts of the kind beloved by modern showmen—causing Lake Galilee to freeze or a giraffe to suddenly appear. Just imagine the effect! There were occasions when His miracles were intentionally provocative, most especially those He did on the Sabbath to challenge the extrabiblical traditions and legalisms of the Jewish leaders. More commonly, His miracles were acts of deep compassion: healing the sick, setting free the demonized, restoring the disabled, raising the dead. His mercy reached to all: men and women, Jew and Gentile, rich and poor, worthy and unworthy. His miracles opened a window into the heart of our God, giving us confidence that, whatever our need, He is willing to respond.

And He is also able. His authority overcame all resistance, whether from the powers of nature, disease, demons, or death. All were subject to Him. He spoke or touched, and storms ceased, disease and disability disappeared, demons fled, and death vanished. He is Lord of all, even though He was truly human. All of these were foretastes of the coming kingdom, where God's Old Testament promises will be fulfilled on the earth, over which the Lord Jesus will rule and reign in person as King.

When John the Baptist was troubled by the fact that the course of events around Jesus wasn't unrolling the way he had expected, he sent messengers to Jesus to ask whether He truly was the Messiah John had proclaimed Him to be. The Lord responded by pointing him to His miracles as signs that the kingdom was already present in anticipation of its final manifestation: "Go and tell John what you hear and see: the blind receive their sight and the lame walk, lepers are cleansed and the deaf hear, and the dead are raised up, and the poor have good news preached to them. And blessed is the one who is not offended by me" (Matthew 11:4–6). His miracles weren't random acts, but anticipations of God's kingdom promises.

Perhaps on behalf of all the disciples, John writes of Jesus, "We have seen his glory, glory as of the only Son from the Father, full of grace and truth" (John 1:14). As we saw in the very first miracle we studied, when Jesus turned water into wine at Galilee, John concludes his account by telling us that Jesus "manifested his glory. And his disciples believed in him" (2:11). Each miracle that followed manifested more of that glory to them, until His resurrection left them all saying, with Thomas, "My Lord and my God!"

(20:28). The primary purpose of the Lord's miracles was to authenticate His true identity and His divine message. It is an astonishing claim that God has become a man. How could that possibly be? Only the miracles could begin to make it evident that Jesus was in a category all by himself. Jesus didn't just *do* miracles, He was a miracle himself. As He declared, "The works that I do in my Father's name bear witness about me" (John 10:25).

The only reasonable response to the cumulative power of Jesus's miracles, crowned by His resurrection, is to bow before Him in worship and wonder. "My Lord and my God!" is the necessary response when we finally understand who He truly is. And in that light, the cross only becomes more astonishing. The One who had all power allowed himself to be taken by sinful men and executed in a travesty of justice. Obviously, the Jewish religious leaders and the Roman authorities could only do what they did because He allowed them to do so. And He tells us why: "The Son of Man came not to be served but to serve, and to give his life as a ransom for many" (Matthew 20:28). "I am the good shepherd. The good shepherd lays down his life for the sheep. . . . I lay down my life that I may take it up again. No one takes it from me, but I lay it down of my own accord. I have authority to lay it down, and I have authority to take it up again" (John 10:11, 17–18). His compassion did not extend only to the physically sick and broken. By dying on the cross, He took sin's penalty for all those who put their faith in Him and bow before Him as Lord and Savior.

As John ends his account of the Lord's life, he directs us to the reason he has so carefully recorded the words and works of Jesus: "Now Jesus did many other signs in the presence of the disciples, which are not written in this book; but these are written so that you may believe that Jesus is the Christ, the Son of God, and that by believing you may have life in his name" (20:30–31). As you have taken this journey through the miracles of Jesus, I hope you have come to recognize that indeed the risen Lord is, in fact, the Christ, the Son of God, who not only did great miracles but did the greatest thing He could: He paid the penalty for our sins so that all who entrust themselves to Him might know they have received the great miracle of forgiveness and eternal life. If you have not done so, even as you put down this book, I invite you to bow your knees to Him in trust, thanksgiving, and worship. The greatest miracle you will ever experience is what Jesus describes as the new birth, which will change not only your present but your eternity as well.

ACKNOWLEDGMENTS

This book would not have been possible without the love, support, encouragement, prayers, and wise input of my wife, Elizabeth. For more than fifty years, we have done life together, and my gratitude to the Lord for bringing her into my life only deepens with each passing year. She is a blessing to me, our children, and our grandchildren, and to a multitude of others who have been loved and served by her.

Thanks are due as well to the believers at Redeemer Fellowship in Loma Linda, California. Helping to plant a church together at this stage in my ministry has been a great privilege, and I am thankful for your warm response, prayerful support, and constant encouragement. I am grateful as well for the gift of family and friends who continue to enrich my life in so many ways.

Thanks also to the gifted team at Our Daily Bread Publishing, who gave me the opportunity to partner with them on this book, a companion to *The Parables: Understanding What Jesus Meant*. Your skills make this book far better than it would have been otherwise.

Supremely, my thanks are due to my Lord and King, "who loved me and gave himself for me" (Galatians 2:20). May this book help those who read it see You more clearly, trust You more deeply, and praise You more profoundly.

Worthy are you to take the scroll
and to open its seals,
for you were slain, and by your blood you ransomed people
for God
from every tribe and language and people and nation,
and you have made them a kingdom and priests to our God,
and they shall reign on the earth.

(Revelation 5:9–10)

NOTES

Introduction: Can We Even Believe in Miracles?

1. See, for example, Peter Carlson, "The Bible according to Thomas Jefferson." *The Humanist*, February 18, 2012, https://thehumanist.com/magazine /march-april-2012/features/the-bible-according-to-thomas-jefferson.

2. Alex Rosenberg, *An Atheist's Guide to Reality: Enjoying Life without Illusions* (New York: W. W.Norton, 2011), xiii.

3. Richard Dawkins, *The Blind Watchmaker: Why the Origin of the Universe Reveals a Universe without Design* (New York: W. W. Norton, 2015), 139.

4. It is beyond the purpose of this book to describe that evidence. However, on the popular level, much can be found in: Gary Habermas and Michael Licona, *The Case for the Resurrection of Jesus* (Grand Rapids, MI: Kregel Publications, 2004); and Lee Strobel, *The Case for Easter: A Journalist Investigates the Evidence for the Resurrection* (Grand Rapids, MI: Zondervan, 2009). There are also more detailed academic treatments, notably: N. T. Wright, *The Resurrection of the Son of God*, Christian Origins and the Question of God Series, Volume 3 (Minneapolis: Fortress Press, 2003); and Michael Licona, *The Resurrection of Jesus: A New Historiographical Approach* (Downers Grove, IL: IVP Academic, 2010).

5. Paul Barnett, *Finding the Historical Christ (After Jesus)* (Grand Rapids, MI: Eerdmans, 2009), 240.

6. C. S. Lewis, *Miracles* (San Francisco: HarperCollins, 1996), 173.

7. Flavius Josephus, *Antiquities of the Jews*, 18:63–64.

8. Graham Twelftree, *Jesus the Miracle Worker: A Historical and Theological Study* (Downers Grove, IL: InterVarsity Press, 1999), 254.

9. Twelftree, *Jesus the Miracle Worker*, 255.

10. Twelftree, *Jesus the Miracle Worker*, 253.

11. Marcus J. Borg, *Jesus, A New Vision: Spirit, Culture, and the Life of Discipleship* (San Francisco: HarperSanFrancisco, 1991), 61.

12. Bart Ehrman, *Jesus: Apocalyptic Prophet of the New Millennium* (New York: Oxford University Press, 1999), 199.

13. N. T. Wright, *Jesus and the Victory of God*, Christian Origins and the Question of God Series, Volume 2 (Minneapolis: Fortress Press, 1996), 187.

Chapter 1: A Sign in the Wine

1. As Emily Thomassen notes, "Nathanael's initial attitude toward Jesus may suggest that Cana was more affluent or cosmopolitan than Nazareth." Emily J. Thomassen, "Jesus' Ministry at Cana in Galilee" in *Lexham Geographical Commentary on the Gospels,* ed. Barry J. Beitzel (Bellingham, WA: Lexham Press, 2017), 75.
2. Craig Keener, *The Gospel of John: A Commentary, Volumes 1 & 2* (2003; repr., Grand Rapids, MI: Baker Academic, 2012), 1:506.

Chapter 2: Supreme Authority

1. Joe Carter, "Survey: Majority of Americans Believe in the Existence of Satan and Demon Possession," The Gospel Coalition, September 23, 2013, https://www.thegospelcoalition.org/article/survey-majority-of-americans-believe-in-the-existence-of-satan-and-demon-po/.
2. Karl Paul, "Why millennials are ditching religion for witchcraft and astrology," *Market Watch*, October 31, 2016, https://www.marketwatch.com/story/why-millennials-are-ditching-religion-for-witchcraft-and-astrology-2017-10-20.
3. The only exception is the healing of a blind man at Bethsaida, who first sees "people, but they look like trees, walking," and the Lord completes the miracle with a second touch (Mark 8:22–26). The fact that Jesus questions the man after the first stage may indicate that this two-stage healing was for symbolic reasons.

Chapter 3: Fish Stories

1. A very helpful description of fishing in Lake Galilee can be found in Carl Laney, "Fishing the Sea of Galilee," in *Lexham Geographical Commentary on the Gospels,* 165–74.
2. Laney, "Fishing the Sea of Galilee," 168, citing *Wars* 3.508–9.
3. Luke here calls it "the Lake of Gennesaret." There are three different names for the lake found in the Gospels: the Sea of Galilee, the Sea of Tiberias (named after the city Herod built on the lake to honor the Roman emperor Tiberius), and the Lake of Gennesaret. The last is a Greek form of Kinnereth, meaning "harp," a name reflecting the fact that the lake is harp-shaped.
4. David Bivin, *New Light on the Difficult Words of Jesus: Insights from His Jewish Context* (Holland, MI: En Gedi Research Center, 2005), 72–73.

Chapter 4: A Portrait of Grace

1. Rodney Stark, *The Rise of Christianity: How the Obscure, Marginal Jesus Movement Became the Dominant Religious Force in the Western World in a Few Centuries* (San Francisco: HarperSanFrancisco, 1997), 155.
2. Cited in Stark, *Rise of Christianity*, 82.
3. Mark records the cleansing of the leper in 1:40–45 and omits the healing of the centurion's servant. Luke records the leper's cleansing in 5:12–16 and the servant's healing in 7:1–10.
4. Moses prayed for his sister, Miriam's, healing (Numbers 12:13), while Elisha was instrumental in the healing of Naaman (2 Kings 5:9–14).
5. Matthew has chosen to collapse the account. Rather than depicting the Jewish intermediaries, he views the centurion as the real speaker through his spokesmen. Luke instead describes the spokesmen. This is not a contradiction, but a different perspective on the story. Matthew is focused on the one-on-one encounter between a Roman official and Jesus, the Messiah.

Chapter 5: First Things First

1. "The details in the story of digging through the roof fits well with the customary roof construction in which long poles spaced about 18 inches apart would have been covered with more slender branches and mud that was rolled each season to pack it together." Elaine A. Phillips, "The Domestic Architecture of Capernaum and Beyond," in *Lexham Geographic Commentary on the Gospels*, 110.
2. I have considered the subject of forgiveness at some length in *Forgiveness: Discover the Power and Reality of Authentic Christian Forgiveness* (Grand Rapids, MI: Discovery House, 2005).

Chapter 6: Storm Lessons

1. Gordon Franz, "What type of storms did Jesus calm: wind or rain?" in *Lexham Geographical Commentary on the Gospels*, 177–78.
2. Franz, "What type of storms did Jesus calm: wind or rain?", 178.
3. Charles Haddon Spurgeon, "The Fruit of the Spirit: Joy," sermon delivered February 6, 1881, *The Metropolitan Tabernacle Pulpit*, vol. 27. (London: Passmore & Alabaster, 1882), 77.
4. J. Weiss, quoted in Alan Hugh McNeile, *The Gospel According to St. Matthew: The Greek Text with Introduction, Notes, and Indices* (1915; repr. ed., Grand Rapids: Baker, 1980), 104.

5. C. S. Lewis, *Prince Caspian: The Return to Narnia,* The Chronicles of Narnia (1951; repr., New York: HarperCollins, 1994), 141.

6. Part of this phrase was ingrained on my memory from a sermon I read or heard. But my memory unfortunately fails to recall its proper source! My apologies to the originator!

Chapter 7: Power Encounter

1. Evidence of this confusion is found in the fact that in Matthew, Mark, and Luke, the Greek manuscripts have variant readings: "Gerasenes," "Gadarenes," or "Gergasenes." The issue of place name is a complex one, but there is no question about the general location of the event, only the term chosen by the gospel writers to describe it.

2. Mark Strauss, *Jesus Behaving Badly: The Puzzling Paradoxes of the Man from Galilee* (Downers Grove, IL: InterVarsity Press, 2015), 58.

3. Matthew 8:28 tells us that there were two men. This isn't a contradiction. When I told my very English grandmother, "I saw the Queen today," I wasn't deceiving her by not mentioning that Prince Philip was there as well.

4. C. S. Lewis, *The Screwtape Letters* (1961; repr., San Francisco: Harper-SanFrancisco, 2001), ix.

5. Strauss, *Jesus Behaving Badly*, 60.

6. Bertrand Russell, "Why I Am Not a Christian," *Why I Am Not a Christian and Other Essays on Religion and Related Subjects* (1927; repr., London: Unwin Books, 1967), 22.

Chapter 8: Helpless but Not Hopeless

1. Burials were carried out the day of death. Matthew mentions that flute players were already present (9:23). "Loud mourning and wailing characterized Jewish wakes. Even the poorest people were required to hire at least two flute players and one wailing woman to perform these services (m. Kethub. 4:4)." Craig Blomberg, *Matthew: An Exegetical and Theological Exposition of Holy Scripture*, The New American Commentary 22 (Nashville, TN: Broadman & Holman Publishers, 1992), 161.

2. Reliable tradition indicates that Peter was the verbal source for most of Mark's gospel. First Peter 5:13 reveals Mark was with Peter in Rome, symbolically referred to as "Babylon" in that letter.

Chapter 9: Lord of the Sufferer and the Sabbath

1. Daniel Trotta, "New York City creates gender-neutral 'X' option for birth certificates," *Reuters*, October, 9, 2018, https://www.reuters.com/article /us-usa-lgbt-new-york/new-york-city-creates-gender-neutral-x-option-for -birth-certificates-idUSKCN1MJ2OP.
2. Yugal Levin, quoted in Trevin Wax, "4 Big Challenges Facing the Church in the West Today," *LifeWay Voices*, January 2, 2019, https://lifewayvoices.com /culture-current-events/4-big-challenges-facing-the-church-in-the-west-today/.
3. Mishnah b. Ned 38b.
4. In addition to the miracle here in Mark 5, see also Mark 1:21–28, 29–31; 3:1–6; Luke 13:10–17; 14:1–6; and John 9:1–16.

Chapter 11: Master of Surprise

1. This oft-quoted statement first appeared in 1943, in the English literary magazine *The Chimera*.
2. Flavius Josephus, *Against Apion*, 1:70–71.
3. Strauss, *Jesus Behaving Badly*, 130.

Chapter 12: But Now I See

1. Rhitu Chatterjee, "Feature: Giving blind people sight illuminates the brain's secrets," *Science*, October 22, 2015, https://www.sciencemag.org /news/2015/10/feature-giving-blind-people-sight-illuminates-brain-s -secrets#:~:text=NEW%20DELHI%E2%80%94Manoj%20Kumar% 20Yadav,first%20few%20months%20of%20life.
2. The five episodes are the healing of two blind men (Matthew 9:27–31); a demonized man unable to see or speak (Matthew 12:22–32); a blind man at Bethsaida (Mark 8:22–26); a man born blind (John 9); Bartimaeus and his companion (Matthew 20:29–34; Mark 10:46–52; Luke 18:35 –43). That there were many others is clear from Matthew 15:30, 31; 21:14.
3. Elaine A. Phillips, "Healing by Living Water at the Pool of Siloam," *Lexham Geographic Commentary on the Gospels*, 370.
4. C. S. Lewis, *The Weight of Glory* (1949; repr., New York: Macmillan, 1980), 92.

Chapter 13: The Death Conqueror

1. The seven "I am" statements of Jesus are: "I am the bread of life" (John 6:35); "I am the light of the world" (John 8:12); "I am the door of the sheep" (John

10:7); "I am the good shepherd" (John 10:11); "I am the resurrection and the life" (John 11:25); "I am the way, and the truth, and the life" (John 14:6); "I am the true vine" (John 15:1).